THE LEGENDARY COWBOY CON MAN

The trouble with legends is sometimes there true

TOUGHTENSE TERRIFIC "AND TRUE"

The last of a breed unique to the twentieth century worked CANADA UNITED STATES AND LATER THE WORLD. THE COWBOY CON MAN PLAYED EVERY CON WITH FIRST SCIENCE LUCK AND SUPERSTITION, MEANING IF IT DIDN'T FEEL RIGHT HE DIDEN'T DO IT. THIS TRUE STORY ENGAGING ACCOUNTS OF TOMMYS LIFE AS A "MAJOR LEAGE HUSTLER   AND SUPER STAR OF THE 21TH CENTURY.

OWNER gangster ways productions Inc-time stamped and Deposit receipt

15

Chapter one

This true story starts with Tommy's father
William Leonard Marks.

20 The mentor and teacher of the legendary Cowboy con man.

They called him (Young Billy)
He grew up in now the ghost town of Armada, located on the east banks of Lake
McGregor called (snake valley). It was tough territory and very segregated from any
25 settlements most families that settled there were running from something, people came
from all over the United States and eastern Canada… a hot bed for Irish and Scottish
gangsters and immigrants.

The area is referred to as Snake valley country of southern Alberta, between the towns
30 of Lomond and Milo Alberta Canada hard country to tame people were ready for
violence because that's what they were running from.
They found a home there with no rules the toughest and smartest ran the country.
The weak were pursed aside.

35   Billy's parents were early homesteaders and were lucky to find a beautiful section of
land in the valleys highest point in Armada.

"THIS IS WHERE IT ALL BEGAN"

40 Young Billy's hand and eye coordination and 'Smart's, were uncanny.
  Billy could make even the hottest tempered man see and think exactly the way Billy

wanted him to. Call manipulation Billy found an old book in Anne, his mother's English

trunk. The book was about the mystic world of manipulation (Billy studied it cover to

cover, Anne brought it from summer set England.

45   The date on the old English book was 1896 old hustler's manual of manipulation.

     And it worked! Even grown men were not a match as Billy seemed to know what they were going to say before it came out of their mouth.

50   Billy concentrated on the art of manipulation, practiced on his mother Anne but
    It never worked. But close. Anne Marks encouraged Billy sometimes she went for Billy's con,
    But she gave it away with a wink Anne studied the book of manipulation away before Billy came along.
55 Strangers never knew what hit them until much later.
    (Billy learned manipulation)
    But Billy soon learned another skill that went hand and hand with manipulation.
    It became his heart ambition and that was a snooker player for the bucks?

60

    The trick was to let the mark win and there was a certain way of losing that gave the mark his thrill of satisfaction thinking he was much better and they all did the same thing very quickly. They put themselves as the best snooker player, it was addicting for the mark.
65 When they got this feeling, it was just like shooting fish in a barrel.
    They had no place to go.

    Billy would clean the mark out before he realized what happened.
    It would take them a few days before the realized what happed?
70

    Billy quickly became ranked number three in the Alberta snooker tour.

    But that ranking wasn't what Billy was after.
    Young Billy was looking to improve his hustling skills more than anything and if he
75 ranked high on the snooker circuit it would give him away with the screamers.

    He was setting up to take all they have.
    Therefore, Billy had to withdraw from the competition in order to hustle for the big bucks then knowing he was one of the best by ranking no three without trying very hard.
80

    Later the older champions told young Billy they liked the kid and if he wants to throw his hat into the ring with the best notorious hustlers Billy has go to Vancouver on the west coast of Canada.

85 It is the biggest port city in Canada and go to the famous Hastings street where Hustlers' from all over the world are there arriving every day, it's a hot spot.

The billiard halls are some of the classiest joints in North America; with thick red carpets and crystal chandeliers.
It is a class act (you can smell the money everywhere).
90
The best in Alberta told Billy most if not all the best hustlers from California stop there.

They are on their way to the Klondike and Alaska gold rush. That's where the money is. Catch them at Hasting, then catch the halters that are coming back from their hustling
95 the gold miners... their pockets are full!

From the famed Seymour Billiards to the Hastings Billiards, there was always a new Diamond Brady", ID Hot stick) trying to make a name for himself and the money that goes with such a distinguished handle after traveling money to the gold rush.
100
It wasn't an easy life-style to say the least but Billy had become accustomed to living on the road.
In Alberta, he hustled enough to purchase a brand-new Ford model-A ford.

105

CHAPTER 2

The year was 1928 Billy took the advice of the older Alberta champions.
Then packed his three best pool cues and then he had to look the part of a class man
110 entering into that big league his best suite.
Then change his mind.
Pack some ranch cloths, his old hat and canvas running shoes.

And for the long journey across the mighty Rocky Mountains, Billy's mother packed a
115 whole sack full of homemade canned goods. Old home made canned beef, beans and homemade cheese, and some hard biscuits.
Billy was on a real hard enduring trip to Vancouver.
Because there were no roads though the Rocky Mountains

120 Not only had the mountains he had very limited amount of cash. Billy had saved up

seven hundred fifty dollars.

There was no room for a mistake!

There was a railway track combined with the someday to come gravel road in parts.

Billy drove the old model -A on to the railway tracks, it fit perfect.

125 Then let a small bit of air out of the tires.

This started at Blair more, the famous crow's nest pass Alberta to Vancouver.

There was only one train a month servicing few towns to the province of British Columbia to Alberta.

The tracks were not finished.

130 Things were going great. Billy never even had to steer,

Billy set the throttle on the old model A as it would follow on its own on the train tracks through the beautiful Rocky Mountains by itself.

Billy relaxed sometimes sleeping while the car followed the train tracks automatically.

135 Billy was on the trip of his life in the back of his mind he could not wait to shoot the best snooker players in the Vancouver, he knows he was the best!?

His mind was racing!

And Billy was going to prove it.

140 But he would play the lame duck and smart-ass country punk both at the same time?

Use his manipulation or anything to win.   Billy was nervous.

Billy ran into parts of the railway not finished however there were temporary track set for the train to cross once a month.

145

If Billy ever was traveling straight into a coming train, he could jump off the tracks quickly to avoid a sure death collision and then take one of many horse trails alongside the tracks until the train passed.

 Then get back on the rails.

150 Billy enjoyed watching the beauty of the valleys after valleys through a wonderful journey it took Billy eight days to get to Vancouver.

Billy was interested in the hobo camps and heard so many stories about and the Chinese who were building the railroad and where they got the expertise to scratch a railway

155 track through the Rocky Mountains and all the stories about the hobo camps.

Billy was welcomed by both a young man from south of the marks homestead in Lomond Mr. dick Teasdale one of Alberta's best boxers.

160 Who was riding the rails to fight and be the champion boxer in Vancouver his name was
A good boxer, Billy seen Dick fights in Calgary. Dick was the best there.

Billy was glad to see Dick and offered him a ride to Vancouver, Dick accepted and then
told Billy he almost suffocated hanging on to the roof of the train car; the locomotive
165 smoke was bad going through that tunnel.
I had to tie my belt to the train car if I passed out from the smoke I would not fall.
Billy shook his head.

Billy said you can 't breathes that and fight.
170 There no smoke in my model T." thanks Billy Mr. Dick said.

There was a hobo camp up ahead, they waved us over and offered us a hot meal.
We accepted. The first hobo camp Billy ever seen

175 Then the hobos fed Billy and Dick.
Then we all set up around a big camp fire, we heard all their stories, then they heard
Billy's and Dicks story, they all had similar stories. They all agreed that we will see both
of you back here trying to get home to Alberta.
Sitting in the hobo camp was exciting, they were all nice people just trying to feed their
180 families. There was no work, it was the times we now know of as the Dirty thirties.

Telling Billy if it wasn't for the Chinese workers we wouldn't have anything to eat
…those Chinese are good people we will never steal anything from the Chinese. They're
too good.
185 Billy loved their stories, but we were on our way at day break.

Billy thought this was his fortune his start in life.

All the hobos shook their heads at Billy and Dick waved to them … Dick saying to Billy
190 they think they we'll see both of us will be back here shortly with our pockets empty!
Billy answered they could be right.

Finally, Billy and Dick came across a real road; this meant they were getting close to a
city or a town.
195 It turned out to be Vancouver.

They quickly found the famous Hastings Street; they drove it up and down. Billy seeing
the pool hall his friends in Calgary told him to go to if he wants to make the big bucks, it

was right in front of Billy the famous" Seymour billiards"

200

Billy's eyes were stuck wide open just looking at the door.
Dick said Billy it's not heaven's door.

Billy answered no but it might be the pearly gates"

205

Dick laugh then said Billy you're trying something, you might not make anything.

Billy you're from a little farm in Alberta (this is the big city) there's hustlers everywhere
from California to Seattle.

210 What makes you think you can beat the best hustlers from California all going to the
Klondike to take the miners gold, even their gold claims.
Then (Dick and Billy looked at each other for a few seconds)

"Billy answered well I don't think that way (I have tested the waters)

215 I can shoot with the best. But thanks for the advice!

Then Billy said to Dick how you are going to beat all the top boxers in this big city of
Vancouver. You're from a small town called Lomond in southern Alberta only two
hundred people and you got beat a few times in the Lomond bar too.

220 Dick said I was drunk.

They both looked at each other then smiled. Billy then said Dick lets win, lets kick
some ass! yes Dick answered let kick ass!
Then Billy and Dick went separate ways (dick went to the water front), that's where

225 boxers hang.

They wished each other good luck.
Then they both had feelings of the adrenalin rush? Gave each other the thumb off their
nose, that mean's good luck.

230

235

240

245

250

WILLIAM LOENARD MARKS

CHAPER 3 (BILLY SET UP)

Billy checked into a nice grand hotel called the BAL Moral Hotel. Three blocks from Seymour billiards.

First thing, Billy ordered was hot water for a bath. Then he ate sea food, then slept for two days.

Billy was well rested and Started watching the new Americans that got off the big ship the fairies from Seattle.

BILLY could tell the slickers the way they were dressed and their jewelry, plus the precious custom stick case's they carried.

Ready for the first stage of his plan,

Billy **was excited; the plan was to canvas all the snooker halls and find out and identify who could do great damage if playing him watch for their expertise.**

Then Billy had to know every shark, and their weaknesses, if there was any. Billy watched their betting habits.

Billy never had enough cash to clean anyone out. Billy had to find a way to bluff and show them he had a lot of cash in the bank.

Billy watched and keeps notes on all sharks and got to know them and their routing. Things like how much they would gamble and how many games they could play before fatigue would set in.

Then most of all the little tricks that could increase Billy's odds of beating them… it helps to know their habits before you play them.

Some sharks if the light dimmed somewhat, they would miss a shot because of the unwanted shadows on the snooker balls and table, the hustlers in Calgary showed Billy a trick.

If you weren't aware of this trick Billy knew you could lose out big time as Billy had learned to grow up on the hustling in Alberta.

It only took Billy less than a second to insert or jam a copper penny into the electric old plug in cord.

It worked every time, it dimmed the table lights and made it harder with more
295   shadows and long shoots, for the older real sharks to see Billy could do this while he racked the balls without anyone seeing him.

Billy was spotting all the sharks.

300   Billy was short of cash only twelve hundred dollars left, not enough to start hustling the big boy's. They would clean me out in a couple games.

Billy had a plan.

The next morning Billy slept good, put his suite on and walked up Hastings Street to Main Street.
305   (The center of Vancouver)

"Billy entered the bank, looked at the marble pillars and floors."

The manager came to welcome him. He introduced himself, Billy did the same, and
310   then asked if he could open a big business account.

Billy was a gold buyer, that supplied London England and the western United States.

Billy explained that there won't be any loan's because cause the gold is sold before
315   I buy it sir, Billy said.

The banker asked a question Billy wasn't ready for. The banker asks where you are storing the Gold Billy.

Billy quickly answered haven't you got the storage for the gold sir.

320   YES, THE Dominion Bank can safely store your Gold Billy.

Great Billy said it take two weeks to hear from London and around the same from the western United States.

Bill then asked if I could get a book of checks that are so fancy they look like bank
325   notes. It helps to do business sir.

The banker said he will print good ones for your business Billy.

The banker then asked… can you make a deposit Billy?

330   Yes, Billy said I can deposit twelve hundred cash from my pocket is that enough sir

until the deposits from London or United States come in.

The banker said you're in business Billy… yes, the dominion bank will cover any overdraft for you Billy marks up to five thousand. Billy said shouldn't need the overdraft but it might come in handy sir, thanks.
The checks will take three to four days.
The bank was conned right in.
It would not take long before everyone in Vancouver would know rich Billy was the spoiled rich kid.

Then Billy made one friend that didn't know too much, but he stayed around looking for a hand out, and told everyone all.

Billy needed to find out about all slickers.
   The hand out:
   Billy watched three-real big sharks and they were outstanding to watch them play on the back table in Seymour billiards.

Billy watched them for five days,

   They were real hustlers with nice suits on and they were defiantly Diamond Brady's for sure.
   There sticks were the best in Vancouver.

Then there were the second string of sharks, there wasn't much difference from them and the diamond Brady's.

Billy was getting ready for his lame duck set up young country bump kin, and Billy played it well.

Billy had a plan he watched a hustler do this in Calgary.

Billy started playing every night with all the want to be hustlers.

Most had big plans and a big mouth to go with them.

Billy found the best player on the want too bee's he had the biggest mouth, just what Billy was looking for someone that knows the big sharks?
He would tell them everything.

370   Billy started playing.
        Billy racked the balls the big mouth told Billy it cost two dollars to play me.
        Billy said how come so much.

        They agreed as the game was happening Billy said, do you know the Waldron
375   Ranch?
        Yes, the mouth said, it's the biggest ranch in Canada.

        Then Billy was setting the stage for the sharks.

380   Billy said that's my Dads ranch, we are rich! Oh, the mouth said, then cleaned the
        table beating Billy.
        Let's shoot another the mouth said, Billy said it's OK to lose.

        I have Twenty-Five Thousand Dollar's in the bank in savings.
385
        The mouth then beat Billy five games strait won ten dollars.

        Billy paid the mouth.
        Then Billy asked… I heard there was real diamond Brady's playing here is there?
390
        Yes, the mouth said, can you take me to watch then tonight please.
        I'll give you five more dollars.
        Yes, the mouths said, give me the five bucks! Billy said you have to introduce me.

395   Yep that's no problem the mouth said. Billy handed the five to the mouth, and out
        on to the street and down to Seymour billiards they went.

        Into Seymour billiards they went and all the way to the back table.

400   There were three well dress men, waiting for an easy mark. They were the same
        hustlers Billy was watching.

        The mouth introduced Billy.

405   Billy stood there with a shit looking grin.

        Then the mouth said Billy is the son of the biggest rancher it the country he is rich,
        and likes to play snooker.

410 And Billy has twenty-five thousand savings in the bank
            The Dominion Bank of Canada
You could see the look on the faces of the three sharks.
Billy had to play it smart, the one shark the best the king of Hastings.
Said Billy it's a real pleasure meeting you.
415

We are only playing around but any time you want a game to come and join us.

Billy said well do you know I am a good, I play out on the ranch.

420 They smiled and said that's good, come anytime.

Billy said thank you Mr. I don't have any cash right now, but I'll come and have
fun with you in a few days.
Then Billy walked away… but on his walk by,
425

 Billy could hear the mouth telling the sharks he just took ten dollars from him, he
can't shoot.
One of the sharks said I figured that.

430 Billy was set up; now Billy had to start sharpening up.
Billy would start in the mornings… no one's around then.

A few days later Billy ran into the mouth, and set him up even more.

435 Billy told the mouth his Dads gold mine just hit big time.

There's more gold there than in all the banks in Canada.

Billy is the son of a multimillionaire!
440 Billy knows this info would get back to the sharks.

Billy only wanted to play the big sharks, not the small timers.
The sharks will come after Billy and try and hit the jack pot!

445 It is working! When Billy went into a restaurant, they all treated him with respect
because of the rumors of him being the son of a multimillionaire.

Billy was starting to live and act like a rich spoiled kid.

But it felt good.

450 The sting was about to begin.

Billy dressed up like a millionaire, purchased a nice suite throwing away his old suite.

The word spread fast!

455 Billy went to the Dominion Bank and his checks were ready. Billy looked at the cashier checks.

They were colored light green with the Canadian mint embalms on each corner.

Billy was waiting for the next step of the con.

460 Billy went straight to Seymour billiards, strolled to the back table where the three sharks hung.

Billy said to the King hustler, I got time for only two games sir… would you play?

The shark said rack the balls Billy.

465

The shark said fifty dollars. Billy asks would you take a check sir I haven't got that much cash with me; I will Write you a check if it's ok sir. The bank is only four doors from here, the dominion bank of Canada. The shark said I take cash. Billy said the bank is just a few doors down the street. It opens at ten tomorrow.

470 But you might not have my check, I might beat you.

The shark said put it in the top pocket.

Billy did.

475 The shark broke the balls and one red went in. then ran three blacks.

Billy shot and missed and easy shot. Then the shark cleared the table.

Then the next game Billy wrote another fifty-dollar check and dropped it in the top
480 pocket.

The shark made short work of Billy winning two games and one hundred dollars.

The shark took Billy's two checks saying are these good?

485 Billy said I would not have written them if they weren't.

The shark said I'll be in the bank in the morning.

The next day the shark entered the Domination Bank and handed the two checks of
490 Billy's to the teller.
THE Bank teller never even looked at Billy's check, and handed the shark one
hundred big ones without looking.

The shark asks how did you know those checks were good mama?
495 The lady teller then told the shark,
Oh, this is one of our very important customer's sirs.

(The shark was satisfied (Billy was rich.)

500

505
VANCOUVER CANADA -HASTINGS, BUSELING PROSPROUS PORT - CITY 1929

BILLY'S -SET UP

510

CHAPTER- 4

This of course was set up just the way Billy wanted it.

515
Now Billy was ready to start the country boy hustle.

Billy was prepared to sell his model a ford and go back to Alberta with all or nothing!

520

Billy slept all day and had a light supper. Before Billy could relax, Billy had to slice up lime and put them over his eyes and cold wet towel over that this would make Billy's eyes clear for at least twenty-four hours.

525 "Young Billy marks age twenty-two"

The word spread fast, everyone thought Billy was a spoiled son of the richest Gold Minor rancher in the territory, a spoiled brat that had everything.

530 And Billy played it Well left, big tips when the right people were around, and play sort of a dummy.
But it was the entire masterful plan to get too the king diamond Brady's.

Every small-time hustler wanted a crack at the spoiled money bags Billy;

535

Billy only had one thing in mind… the three sharks, the kings of hasting.

Billy was just hours away from either cleaning them out or selling the model A to get back to Alberta with his tale behind him.

540

He had a book of checks in his suite pocket…and the king shark knows the checks are good!

It was around eleven.

545 Time to get ready for the biggest hustle of Billy's life. Billy had to start shooting and get as sharp as he can.

He washed his face with soap and put his suite on this time it was for real. Billy was about to join the best sharks in the world or go back to the ranch and work

550 cattle.
Billy's heart was beating fast.

Billy kept noticing a young man watching him quite regularly… he set just a couple of booths from Billy.

555

Billy always watched, you never know!

It was eleven thirty at night on Hastings Street, and truly was alive.

560   Billy stopped in front of Seymour Billiards, took a deep breath and said to himself,
      Billy marks, you're the best snooker player on the planet no shot is too hard.

      I will beat these sharks out of everything they have; they won't know what hit
      them.
565   Then Billy entered. Walked straight to the three Diamond Brady's, they were all
      glad to see young Billy.
      And wondered what Billy wanted.
      Before Billy would not play with them but this time that's what Billy was there for.

570   Just like a gun fighter, he was there to challenge them, but still acting like a simple
      spoiled brat saying the stupidest things a real snooker player would never say.

      Billy knows which one was the real Diamond Brady… that's who Billy talked to
      first. Billy wanted the big boy, the champ and his hottest stick!
575
      Bill quickly threw a nickel on the table and challenged.

      They starred smiling.
      You could see their greed it was making Billy look like a roast turkey, ready to be
580   eaten up! All Billy needed to do now was offer up the cranberry sauce.

      Billy smiled… let's start with one dollar a game. The shark laughed and said boy
      you can't play here for no dollar.
      Then Billy stood there with a shit eating grin and asked, well I never played the big
585   boys before, tell me how much do you guys play for.

      The shark said son, it will be $50 a game.

      Billy's eyes opened wide and said slowly… OK maybe one game.
590
      The shark said boy put you're fifty in the top pocket, I will match it.

      As they flipped the coin Billy lost the flip.

595   The shark smiled as Billy racked the balls. Billy racks them tight.

The shark was surprised when the balls stayed together,

The first thing Billy did was knock the chock off the table it fell on the thick red
600 rug.
     Billy quickly put his finger in his mouth and it was wet with his saliva, then Billy
     put his wet finger in the chock this made the chock slippery. When the shark
     chocked his cue, it made his tip slippery, so he could not control his shots… this
     would throw his control off.
605

     He would shoot harder to get shape, and in a few minutes when it dried it would be
     fast this would throw him off again.

     Then Billy used his own chock, out of his suite pocket.
610 The shark used the table chock only once.
     But that was enough to do the trick.
     The shark missed his first shot.
     Then Billy shot a red in and got perfect position on the black, and then Billy ran
     five more blacks.
615

     When Billy felt the shark hooked, the shark was surprised and did not believe his
     eye's… the shark missed again, his queue was still wet.
     Billy then lined up the next shot, it was a risky shot but Billy wanted to turn the
     match on to full shootout match.
620 Billy put on some inside spin on the cue ball and whacking it hard making it, then
     ran the table.
     Their first game and Billy's plan was working,
     Billy now knows he could beat the shark.
     But this made the shark think Billy was stupid with no experience and got lucky.
625

     The next game the shark said look at Billy and said I haven't got much time.

     I have a date with a real shark!… just came here from California, so let's play for
     some bucks or get out of here.
630 the shark said you got twenty-five thousand in the bank… let's play one more time
     and play for five thousand, or stay away from me boy.

     Billy had the stage set and the shark thinks he can win.

635 Billy worked the shark like this. Billy said I'll put up (twenty-five hundred) too your (Five thousand) you give me two to one.

Billy then said I can't beat you.

640 I just want to tell everyone I played you.
The shark said yes and was smiling, then he said country boy, put your twenty-five hundred in the pocket. Billy replied after you put your five thousand. They both put their cash and Billy put a check for twenty-five hundred in with the sharks five thousand.
645

It was Billy brick the shark racked them tight.

A crowd were starting to gather and that stranger that was following Billy for the last week were there watching Billy.
650

Billy broke the balls only two red balls broke out.
But Billy played a hook on the top end of the table leaving the shark... he could not see a ball.
The shark tried to play a safety but left Billy a red to the corner,
655

Billy made that and got shape on the black.

Billy put lots of side juice of the queue ball and made his shot, breaking the balls out spreading them all around the table.
660

It was all she wrote from there on... Billy cleared the table.

The crowed was talking... what a lucky bunch of shooting.

665 Now Billy was in the driver's seat.

The shark made a big mistake, he didn't know how to take this country bumpkin...was he lucky or did the shark getting conned?

670 The other two Diamond Brady's gathered with the King shark.

They all agreed the kid was lucky.
Try him again they said.

675 OK kid the king shark said… let's play again.

   Billy said with a smart alick manner, do you have any money?

   The shark said let's play for two thousand…Billy said why is that all you have?
680 Smiling.
   The shark was mad! His eye's and that look!

   Billy said I will play for five thousand… strait up even!
   Billy smiled with confidence!
685 The three sharks went into a meeting and the other two seen a chance to double
   their money knowing their friend was much better than this spoiled brat kid. They
   offered their friend a deal, they want in and they would cover the three thousand
   you put up your two thousand… let's take every cent the kids got!

690 The game was on five thousand.

   Only the king shark was short five hundred he pulled a fancy case out and opened
   it.
   It was the diamond Brady's champion ship queue! he said… Billy is this worth five
695 hundred, it's a pure pear handle with two, two hundred carrot purple sapphires on
   it, worth at least one thousand.
   Billy looked at the Pearl handle and the purple sapphires sparkled.

   Billy said let me look at it please.
700

   Then Billy said your short five hundred.
   Yes! the shark said. Billy said you have a deal.

   Thanks kid, but you're a long way from owning the queue son.
705

   It's just on hold for a few minutes. Billy looked the shark strait in his eye and said
   are you sure?
   All three diamonds Brady's were in and their eyes were nervous even burned.
   But Billy thought this is better than he expected… if I win I have cleaned out all
710 three shark's kings of Hastings.

Billy said you're on, but then said do you want to up the bet I have more money?

715 Billy directed this to the other two sharks to see just where they were.

That surprised them suddenly, they knew they were being hustled.

720 Billy became the aggressor.

Then one diamond Brady asked who the hell is you?

Billy said (nobody.)
725
Daddy has a big ranch.

Then they emptied their pockets they had $1500.00 more.

730 They now looked worried.
Billy matched the bet. The game was on!

However, during the past hour or so while Billy was playing the king shark the word spread fast up and down hasting street and commercial there was well over
735 two hundred want to be hustlers or spectators all thinking that the kid had bitten off more than he could chew.

Nevertheless, there hadn't been excitement like this around for week's! One hustler said we really need a change… Someone too show these hot sticks that there is
740 always someone better somewhere down the road.

The important flip of the coin.

Billy called tails and the coin went into the air and landed it was a tail.
745
Winning the brake was important.

played it smart, shooting real soft with just the perfect weight ticked off the outside red, not backing out a ball and hooked the shark behind the yellow up at the far
750 end.
the shark was getting frustrated this happened every time Billy shot, then the

shark finally took a chance and tried to make a red far away long shot and missed.

Leaving Billy, a chance to do real damage
755   Billy not only did real damage.
  Billy ran the entire table.

Putting all three sharks on the street with nothing but a tarnished reputation!

760 The sharks wanted to know who Billy was; no one can shoot like that and didn't come from nowhere, who you are you they demanded.

Billy said nothing, but standing there witnessing the sting was a newspaper reporter.
765 Who watch and witnessing the whole hustle without saying a word!

Then interrupted and handed a paper he had in his hand, and he showed the three sharks.
This young man is not only one of the best in Alberta he ranks number three on the
770 Alberta snooker tour.
  His handle is (Young Billy Marks)

The three hustlers looked at Billy in shock, a few seconds later they shook Billy's hand.
775 They all agreed Billy played the best con with class they ever seen or heard about.

It was a pleasure being hustled by the king shark said I think Billy will be one of the best of all the hustlers… his set up I never seen it until he had me on the ropes, then it was too late.
780

Billy then asked do your gentleman have any startup money.

They all said nope you cleaned us out!
It took us a year to save that much cash one said… I could have purchased a house
785 with the money.

Billy gave each back two hundred to start up again.

They thanked Billy and gave him the salute of the hustlers left finger across the
90 nose, and then got away from Billy quickly.

They never wanted to see him again! The king hustler then said… Billy you can keep that pearl handle with those purple sapphires, I am never playing you again!

795 Billy had finally made his mark the word was out. Billy couldn't get a game with anyone.
The con was over Billy could relax.

The sharks had to start over somewhere other than Vancouver.
800

Billy had to leave Vancouver if he was to set up another hustle.
No one would play Billy for anything.

THE GREAT WARF ROBBERY OF 1929
805 # Chapter 3

The young man that seemed to be watching Billy, was setting next to Billy eating ham and eggs and coffee, this time the stranger talked to Billy, he said well Mr. young Billy you sure conned the cones last night.

810 I kind of figured that but never said anything like that before.

Billy said thank you.
I was conning them but really didn't know if it would work.

815 The stranger said my name is Sammie and requested to join Billy.

Yes, Billy said, join me… let's eat together.

Sammie was talking small talk just to figure Billy out.
820 Then Billy asked if he would be interested in some big money. Billy asks what's the deal is.
Sammie leaned over close to Billy and said… I know we can easily take at least one hundred and fifty thousand out of an old warehouse with very little problems.

825 When the ships unload their cargo the Warf warehouse holds the cash until Friday.

Then Saturday morning deposit it in the bank.

830   There's 0nly one old man there at night with a Billy club.
But we need a fast car to get out of Vancouver... how fast that can model A go Billy?

Well Billy was thinking around forty...
835   No horses will be able to catch us, maybe at first it takes a while to get that steed up, the horses could catch us.
Billy then said I am buying a new 1930 ford it will go almost fifty-five mph and fast!

840   Billy said I am interested but only one thing... nobody gets hurt and I want half the money.
Sammie said no. Billy there is another partner, he is old Frank. He just got out of hard labor prison.
So... one third and all you need to do are drive the car.
845

It's a deal Billy said... but I want to go with you to watch this before we do it.

Sammie said at twelve tonight.
I'll come to your hotel, we will go check it out and you will see.
850

OK Billy said... I'll be ready.

Sammie came at nine thirty, and Billy was sleeping lightly.

355   Billy was on his feet on the first knock, open the door and Sammie said let's have a late lunch at the Oval tine restaurant... very popular joint. Ok, out the door they went.

Billy, we have six days' then it's on.
360

OK Billy said again nobody gets hurt and I am in.

Sammie chose a booth in the back and set there said this is private, then ordering two cups of Joe.
65   On every second Friday, the warehouse takes in untold amount of merchandise off the ships.

They hold this for ten days.
 While the buyers of the products take their last load and then pay for the merchandise.
870 That's when we make our move. They leave the warehouse safe holding approximately one hundred thousand or more!

That safe is nothing for McCauley to open.
The wells Fargo generally collect the money every second Friday at nine Pm.
875

Guaranteed we're after the cash.
 No one will get hurt.
 Billy said well I will finish the deal on my new touring 1930 ford coupe it goes much faster.
880 Let's go watch the set up at the warehouse.

 Billy and Sammie watched all night.

It was just like Sammie said.
885

Sammie told Billy that old Frank the safe cracker was one of the best in the business. Sammie said now with you and your fast car, we have a good crew.

Please go get that new ford coupe.
890 If it goes faster up to 55 M P H. around fifty-five, that's fast!

 OK Billy said one more week. And Billy please stay away from those billiard halls please, is quiet and out of the scene.

895 I am going to relax and maybe there's a nice lady Sammie told Billy, you better watch those ladies around here, they will Conn you out of your pants!

 Billy said yep, I better get ready for next week.

900 I'll have that ford coupe... even it costs me allot of money to boot!

 Seven hundred and fifty dollars…
 I'll make the deal.

905

Billy's Getaway Car 1929

1930 Cabriolet
Dave and Carol Habersang

910   Billy showed Sammie the gold 1930 ford, it was the only one sold in Vancouver. Sammie said show me the take-off speed it's got... Billy said OK, hold on!

    Billy stopped at the corner of main and Hastings's, leaned over and told Sammie hold on! You never seen anything like this... revved the motor and had it in bull low, popped
915 the clutch the front wheels lifted off the street about two inches! Billy changed gears to second, then too third within two blocks! The ford's speed was thirty-five, then climbed to forty shortly after that hit fifty M P H.!!! Sammie yelled stop Billy this car is faster than a bullet!!!
  Billy stops.

920

Sammie said man this car flies! Hope we never half to go that fast ever again.
Billy then said there's a side street just off the water... I'll park there and we will walk through the warehouse, leave out the back door, then nobody should see us leave.

925 Sammie then said we meet tomorrow night then when all the merchandise is sold out of the warehouse, the safe will be empty so tonight is it! Get some sleep Billy. Sammie also told Billy that big Frank the safe cracker's name is really Mr. McCauley; he goes by Frank because everyone knows that name McCauley.

---

930   Sammie watched Billy's expressions getting excited. McCauley is one of the best safe crackers in the business, and then Sammie told Billy they both would come to Billy's hotel at ten thirty tonight. Billy said he would make sure the tires were OK and will be full of gas. I will have five gallons extra. I will be ready Billy said …see you tonight at 10:30.

935

Every night there was a beat cop, an old English bobby that did his rounds. He walked by the warehouse around ten, then in one hour or sometimes two hours again, checking the warehouse doors. We were all ready to go, there was the same old guard inside watching over the safe, but all he had was a Billy club.

940

We were just across the street; we walked to the side of the warehouse just around the side so the guard cold not sees us. Then Sammie through a rock and knock on the door, we could see the guard looking at the front door… then Sammie through another rock, the old guard came to the door opened it and yelled… you kids get out of here!

945

That's when Sammie and big McCauley grabbed the guard from behind. The two of them pulled a hold over the guard and tied him up, then dragged him inside and put him in the back room. The guard never saw anyone. It was then time for Mr. McCauley to show his expertise. He talked while he was working he said, the trick with a lot of safe

950 was getting the first layer of steel to bend enough to get a large tipped chisel in… once the tool could breach the front of the safe it wouldn't take long before it would peel away like an orange!

955 Billy's help with a pry bar holding the steel up so McCauley could take a better bit; the lip of the safe plate was peeling off like butter. In fifteen minutes, the safe top was peeled open. Sammie and Macaulay had four sacks full of money in their hands, then that English cop knocked on the door calling the warehouse guard for something.

960   Billy started first, then Sammie and McCauley ran behind Billy out the back door, threw the sacks of money in the back-rumble seat, and Billy started the ford. Just then the English cop came around the corner.

  Billy took off! The cop was yelling stop you criminal bastards!!!, and before the ford
965 could get enough speed up the English cop jumped onto the side running board of the ford trying to arrest us… The ford went around the corner, speed was picking up and Sammie punched the English cop in the face.

The cop fell off the running board on to the street at the speed of thirty miles per hour.
Billy poured on the speed; there were around ten,

970   Foot cops chasing them… plus two armed cops on horseback!

The ford now was leaving them all behind and opened five blocks.

Sammie knew the roads they drove for hours.

975

It was starting to get light out, Billy asked where are we Sammie?

Sammie said we are in a little town called Chilliwack;

980   This is where the gravel roads end Sammie said.

But there are the railway tracks in the valley.
He pointed at the train tracts.

985   We pulled around the back of some trees and stopped.

Sammie and McCauley said let's split the money and go in separate directions.

They had three piles, they were counting the cash… the stack of cash was so big they
990   had three stacks for each of them.
The total amount for each was $47.000.00 each.

Sammie said we better be real quiet about this, the total is (one hundred and forty-one
thousand) we are rich!!!
995   We can all retire Sammie and McCauley said.

McCauley said I am going south to the United States... And we better keep moving! I
bet the heat is on big time.

1000   Sammie asked, can I come with you Mr. Retired McCauley?

Yes, McCauley answered… come we will live like kings in that place they call
California!

1005   Both Sammie and big McCauley said, you're the best partner we ever had Billy… where
are you going?? Your welcome to come with us south.

Thanks Billy said. I am on my way back to Alberta. McCauley told Billy better make some distance between you Vancouver and fast!

1010

Billy and they shake hands. McCauley and Sammie started walking over the mountain. Sammie told McCauley the United States is only around five-mile's south and then we are safe. Let's go.

1015

CHAPTER 4

Billy drove off to get that new ford on the track as fast as possible.

1020 Bill was on the railway tracks in a few minutes and set the speed as fast as the car would go and stay on the tracks around thirty-five M P H.
Quickly on his way back to Alberta never stopped Billy. He slept as the car automatically followed the tracks. Billy was scared, putting as many miles away from Vancouver as he could.

1025
Billy had made around fifty-five thousand. Billy was one of the rich young men in Alberta, this money was big.

Billy could never let anyone know how much money he had or how he got it.

1030
He felt somewhat guilty. Billy never forgot the adrenalin rush, it was the thrill of his life.

Billy reached fort McLeod and then turned north to Claresholm.

1035 Billy was thinking of gifts for the family driving through Nanton then turned east to Vulcan.
This is where Billy stopped for gas and gifts to buy for the whole family.

Evan Groceries…
1040 His two sisters and Billy's four brothers, and mother and the boss Tommy marks senior, Billy's father.

He could not wait to see the family. They were so happy to see Billy and noticed the new car. Little brother Stanley went and played drive the car, sitting behind the steering

045 wheel.
 Annie, Billy's mother after hugging Billy said, all right why you have stayed all winter over in Vancouver and just what you got into Billy?

Oh mom, Billy could not tell mom anything about the hustle or the Wharf robbery.
050

But Billy just smiled as mom rambled on.

Not getting any info from Billy?

055 Soon after Billy's arrival home,
 Billy started putting together a large parcel of land, buying out big ranchers and small making one of the biggest ranches in the territory and farm land. Billy pushes one thousand head of cattle;

060 Billy had thirty-six square miles of ranch and farm land.

Billy called it the 7H Ranch between the towns of Lomond and Milo southern Alberta Canada.
Billy's favorite area he ever seen was the prairies were Billy was raised, the rolling hills
065 of southern Alberta.

The Rocky Mountains were very nice but the rolling hills the prairies were Billy's home.

070

75

"TWEENTY YEARS LATER"
CHAPTER -5

1080   Bill Marks was one of the biggest farmers and ranchers in the Vulcan County, with a net worth of twenty million.

    With the start up from the hot Diamond Brady's cash, and the great Warf robbery that No one was ever caught for, the greatest robbery in Canadian history.

1085

    The Great Warf Robbery of 1929 Plus the culverts 'Identity and ware bouts is a mystery to this day?

    Plus, Bill marks was crowned The King Diamond Brady Snooker shark, Hottest Stick in

1090 Baltimore United States back in the year of 1933.

    Now Old Bill had four children... the oldest Doreen, second Leonard, third Gwen, and last but not least... (Tommy)
    Bill had everything... kids all educated. Old Bill never had anyone formed like him.

1095   Bill said to himself I am going to teach Tommy the trick of a hustler better then myself.

1100

1105

1110

The making of the legendry cowboy con man

15

I am going to teach Tommy my youngest son the ropes, the Hustlers game. Bill had a Regulation size snooker table in the basement. Old Bill thought maybe not. I should get Tommy into sports or something like most the kids his age was doing.

20

But Bill said my youngest boys going to be my legacy.
I'm going to teach him the hustler's game and how to trick people and win!

From age three Tommy was crawling on top of the regulation size snooker table using a stick Bill had fashioned out of an old oak tree in the back yard.

25

It was the funniest thing, it couldn't have been more than two feet long.

At five, old Bill continued to teach Tommy, now how to put spin on the cue ball making it look like magic.

1130   When bill would shoot with tommy watching,

Tommy was now using a small cue.

1135   Bill showed Tommy how to put back spin on the cue to get shape on the next shot.

Teaching Tommy, old Bill would go to the trouble of setting up a small table with Tommy and sit with Tommy and have tea.

1140   Then Bill would tell Tommy the stories about how to make people think they were better then you. Bill told Tommy, if you let them win and you get disappointed at your shooting, there is a way to make people get so thrilled when you pay them, they are addicted and they get a felling there just allot better then you… then when the bet is big enough when you finally beat them.

1145

They know for a fact they're still better then you.

Then that's when you remove that from them plus their money.

1150   Think Tommy how can you make someone think they're better then you? … that is something we will work on.
Dad's stories would make little Tommy's red hair stand up on the back of his neck.

The dangers and what to look out for (And the art of the con) Dad said Tommy set them
1155   up without them even knowing it.
Tommy that's how it's done play indecent country boy all the way it works Tommy people always think they're smarter than a country bunking?

Then old bill started showing little Tommy the art of the sleight of hand.
1160   Old Bill would take a coin quarter and slip it into his little finger and the coin would smoothly move through bills fingers until it was setting on his thumb.

Then it would disappear magically right before your eyes Bill showed Tommy how it was done, and told Tommy to practice this.
1165

It didn't take long before Tommy could do the disappearing act better then Bill.

Tommy was a natural pool player and the sleight of hand.

170   Old Bill was doing everything to build Tommy confidence. Everything Tommy was learning was getting easier for Tommy.
Bill only had to show Tommy once and Tommy was getting far more interested in magical things.

175   Tommy at age seven would play tricks on mother Viola (Donily) by making thing's she was shining disappear before her eye's. Viola would say Billy your teaching Tommy some of your old tricks.
Now Bill you better not teach Tommy that stuff! Then she played the game with Tommy by saying, I know you have that. In your pocket then mom stuck her hand in Tommy
180   pocket, it was empty.
Then mom said Tommy you put it back right now.

So, Viola had to go into Tommy's other pockets and then find the ornament, then tell Tommy get out of here.
185

Viola sounded mad but she wasn't, she was so proud of Tommy.
Bill told Tommy he was going to stay with an old friend of his for-a while.

In a few days Dad took Tommy to an old carnival magic acts. They were traveling with
190   horse and carriage.
 Dad knows the old hobo many years before.
 Dad and the hobo were friends.
They met many years ago. The hobo looked at Tommy and said is this young man you want me to teach the sleight of hand?
195

Bill said I want Tommy to learn from the best, that's you. Old Bill told the old hobo I want Tommy to learn your magic for one reason, it in stores confidence and sometimes Tommy is short of that… he is almost his own enemy, please teach himself confidence.

200   Please, will you teach him all your tricks?

 How long if Tommy learns fast, the hobo said it will take a while around two months, Bill smiled and said how much do you need to spend lots of time with Tommy?

05   The hobo said oh it will take lots of time, how about $200.dollars?... then looked at Bill.
 Bill reached into his pocket and gave the hobo $500.00. Will that do Mr. Hobo? Bill said.

The hobo said thanks Bill… you always help if you could, thank you.

1210

I'll do a good job, but why are you doing this the hobo asked?
Then old Bill told his friend,
I have four children, three of them are already educated the proper way and are doing great.

1215 But I want Tommy to be my legacy.

Be a hustler, one of the greatest with class.

I am going to groom Tommy into a real gentleman.

1220

Now don't you remember me, I was never trained and I hustled everyone.

(YES, YOUNG BILL THE" HOBO" SAID I REMEMBER)
Ok the hobo answered" I will give you my word I'll help with the gentleman act and the

1225 confidence.
Old Billy said I remember your con games, you were the best!

OK, Bill said get out Tommy, you're staying with Mr. Hobo.

1230 Bill said bring Tommy back when he is ready.

Dad met the hobo years ago and they were very good friend's Tommy could tell.

Dad then told the old hobo to tell Tommy about how classy you were and the thinks you

1235 invented for every con you pulled off.

You played banker politician

Even lord from England with a perfect accent please help me with Tommy.

1240

The old hobo was excited and said Bill, I'll do my best.

And then gave Bill the finger across his nose.

1245 Just before Dad left, he said to Tommy… someday you will use these skills.

Mr. Hobo and I taught you... this is what you need to know.

Tommy practiced shooting snooker and the sleight of hand it's up to you if you're to
sharpen your skills.
　Dad then said maybe you will be dressed in a tuxedo somewhere far away on a big Con.

(With a beautiful woman)
　Tommy my boy dad was smiling?
Tommy answered.
　Dad this sleight of hand Dad it will give me something to think about how to make
people think it's there but now it's gone. Tommy then said I now have lots to think
about? Old Bill then told Tommy it will teach you to focus and how to focus.

CHAPTER 6

"This is the true story of the legendary
(Cowboy con man)"
Life experiences with engaging accounts and Tommy's exclusive style.

According to the cowboy con man
Tommy Marks Donily he never did a con just for the money;

It was more for the excitement or the thrill of the game!

That rare con in which the man's own greed is what makes the scam a success.
The con game is a unique form of art and it requires a shit load of patients from the
man pulling one off.
　Hardly a man knew it better than the Con Man Tommy Marks Donily
THE REAL COWBOY CON MAN

If a con is done well most people most of the time even the victim himself doesn't
even know he's been had.
　Until the Con man is halfway out of the country.

　It's Important that the Cowboy con man play it loose as though whatever gaff or
plot he's portraying was the exact truth.

As they say, "act like you own the place and that's what others will think"

1285 Tommy say's be the cock of the walk.

Fifteen years' latter Bill marks ranch:
Bill was one of the richest in the Vulcan County.

1290 After a good life of having family and friends, Bill had completed almost everything
he set out to do except one thing. That was young Tommy and if the work Bill put
into him worked or not Bill wondered if he might have sent Tommy down the
wrong road.
What if Tommy got hurt or isn't good enough to see the other con's in the big
1295 city… there is all different kinds of hustlers, hope Tommy can smell them coming.

His son Tommy had been groomed for the role of a number one hustles with class.
Perfect gentleman all Tommy had to do was improve his own skills his way and
Only Tommy can do that. (Bill was worried)
1300
Old bill always told Tommy to open the door for your mama and all ladies when
you can Tommy.
Then Bill told Tommy ladies are beautiful and need to be respected and loved.

1305 Bill then said, "you will learn about love Tommy" Love can hurt and save you both
at the same time.
Tommy one thing you don't ever fall in love and be a fool some women do that.
Leave that for the suckers.
Tommy watches out for the wrong kind of woman they will play you.
1310 Trick you don't be hurt by them.
It's all in the game with those kinds of women, they will hurt you take everything.
Tommy, you get a nice girl? Like your mother.
Tommy you're a country boy, lots of city girls will con you or try,
Bill winked and smiled.
1315 Tommy listened to every word.
But it's a lot of fun Tommy you will find that out.
Some girls have power over you for a short time.
Bill smiled.
But I figured it out quickly without any advice.
1320 The kid was a natural!

Young Tommy hit the pool halls throughout Alberta as a teenager and earned
quite a reputation for himself.

325 But old Bill didn't pay him much attention.
Until one-day Tommy and old Bill met in the town of Vulcan at the pool hall.

Old Bill was going to show the kid a few things for real, this was going to be one
more lesson for Tommy.   Bill was there to kick young Tommy's ass.
330 (They had a game and what a game it was.)

Tommy told father Bill to rack the balls anyway he likes.
Old Bill said no Tommy you rack them son.

335 Bill said, I want to see if you have learned anything.

OK Tommy said to himself… I've glued the balls together tight.

Tommy did exactly what old Billy showed him fifteen years ago.
340
Old Bill seen that impossible rack.

There was no way of braking out anything.

345 Then old Bill told Tommy… ok you break them.

Tommy looked at his father he was standing there with the Diamond Brady cue
with the pearl handle and the purple sapphires pool stick that he won from the big
Diamond Brady. Dad pulled off the big hustlers in 1929. In his hand's it looked like
350 Dad was there to kick my ass.

Old Bill saw what Tommy did with the rack and quickly said to Tommy "Go
ahead brake that racks you set up for me" Give it your best shot,"

355 Tommy answered oh no it's your brake.

Dad said it's all yours in a match we always have a mutual person racking the
balls so tommy said you brake the balls let's get on with this quit stalling Tommy.

360 OK Tommy said ok.
Then went and looked on to the wall and found the biggest heaviest cue he could
find.

Lined up and tried to hit the third ball on the right side of the rack.

1365

Tommy hit using the old lumber queue as hard as he could and it hit the rack and bounced in to the air.
Tommy sunk one red in the corner pocket.
Then Tommy changed queues and went for the black a risky shot a sharp cut.

1370

Old bill was getting ready for his turn.
Old bill though that shot was impossible to make.

But the black fell.

1375   Tommy just made two almost impossible shots.

Then Tommy ran the whole table never gave old bill a shot.

(Bill was stunned!)

1380   All the hustlers looked and started talking that was the best shooting they ever seen.
Old Bill turned his back on Tommy and tipped up the glass of beer and drank it down then walked over to Tommy grabbed Tommy's hair and hugged Tommy and kissed him on the forehead.

1385   Son old Bill said you can run like a dear and you're so sharp you can tell what people are going to say before they even open their mouth.
I've seen it many a times'.

And now I see your one of the best snooker players in the world.

1390

(What else is in their Tommy my boy what else my boy)?

Then old Bill decided to pass the torch on right there.

1395   Bill said Tommy here is the pearl handled purple sapphire Diamond Brady the hottest stick in North America many champions owned it. I could feel their sprits.
It's yours Tommy. Not without giving Tommy some advice.
Old bill told Tommy never show the Diamond Brady stick until you're playing for the big or real cash game and the cash is in the pocket.

1400

Then OLD Bill WHISPERED INTO TOMMY'S EAR.

You will have to go make your mark soon Tommy!

405

"You're wasting your time around here" Old bill said "I will show you where to go when it's time "I'll give you a map to follow of hot places to hustle.

410

Chapter 7

The ranch was rolling hills located on the east side of Lake McGregor known as Snake Valley.
 Prairie with the most beautiful especially in the spring when Tommy spent most of

415

His time riding his saddle horse out to check the cattle through the prairie hills.

There were Foxes darting in front of him and coyotes and mule deer with their big ears were seen on a regular basis.

420
 Even the odd wolf from time to time

The wild flowers the crocuses and even the cactus had nice blue and red blooms reminding one of their own little slice of heaven.

425   Tommy was one of the top cowboy 's on the southern Alberta ranches.

But the reason for that was due to having one of the best cow-working horses under Tommy and Tommy had a reputation for being one of the best with the Lariat.

430   Though the north part of the ranch there were beautiful small lakes with Ducks, Geese and even swans
It made the north of our ranch a personal part of Tommy's own Garden of Eden.

Tommy would spend lots of his time up there it was nice.

435

Tommy then went to work riding the hills so he could see every cow.

We had around fifteen hundred head of cows.

1440   **Then came the branding of the calves**

We had to round up all fifteen hundred cows with their calves.

The heard was quite a site the big heard was strong out over a mile long it was a
1445   **site Tommy would never forget.**

With a large heard of cattle there was lots of bailing, putting up feed for the winter months, the winters were long and cold.
Tommy and Brother Leonard would put up over one hundred thousand one
1450   **hundred pound bales up every year by hand.**

Lots of work most ranches had a crew of ten ranch hands to put up half of that but the old man Bill made us tough he said.
We both could handle just about any type of action that came our way!
1455

We were down to the last thousand bales left to stack.

Then the rain came can't stack bales in the rain.
Tommy felt like playing, having a night out.
1460

Tommy bathed and put on his new cowboy hat and new boots his silver and gold belt buckle not to mention a diamond ring.

Then drove to the big city of Calgary to the liveliest night club in the city.
1465

It was called the Ranch man's steak house and bar.
And what a place it was!
It was full all the time rocking!
You could see the neon flashing sign at least twenty miles out of the city!
1470

After working hard just seeing the sign while driving in would make you excited.
The parking lot was always full Tommy had to park all the way in the back of the lot.
There was a part of the bar called the saddle room. It was there the band played
1475   **until three every morning... it was county rock.**

Tommy needed a beautiful woman... riding, looking at cattle, and putting up winter feed just didn't take the place of a pretty woman.

480   Tommy was standing at the bar, and there she was.

        She was so beautiful she had that glow of a ready lady with a fair complexion with
        a godly look.
        She had a little tinge of red hair.
485   And developed full body everything a man could wish for. Wow!

        Tommy asked her to dance, she accepted.

490   We stayed on the dance floor for five songs in a row, we had lots of conversation
        and naturally got real close… it was right.

        She told Tommy she was not married or going out with anyone.

495   Then we went to the shooter bar, she ordered a b52 Tommy said the same.

        Her name was Marilyn. She asked what about you cowboy. have you a wife or
        girlfriend?
        Tommy told Marilyn that his wife died two years ago and this was the first time he
500   left the house other than to work.

        But he spent every second he could with her when she was on her death bed during
        the last sixty days of her life he even was hand feeding her.

505   But she passed away in his arms. He never left her.

        Marilyn listened to Tommy's heart-breaking story and felt sorry for Tommy and
        said you're true to your lady, then aren't you?

510   Tommy looked with puppy eyes and said, once I give my devotion, Tommy is loyal
        to the end!

        Plus, in Tommy's training, he practiced making real tears instantly at the right
        moment.
515   Then Tommy played the part of thinking of his dead wife and the tears started to
        run down Tommy's cheek.
        Yes, Tommy said I have been faithful to her for two years now.

Tommy then told Marilyn that she was the first woman he talked to since her death

1520 and my wife died in my arms.

Marilyn and Tommy had three more shooters.

Then it was exactly the right time to kiss the beautiful lady.

1525 They both locked their arms around each other and embraced for it seemed
perfect.
We set in the back of a big booth. We had to share the booth, it was dark just out of
the lights.
We shared with four strangers.

1530

In the dark booth Marilyn leaned over with her two big breasts pressed them
against my chest meaning it felt magic she was mine at least for the night.

Tommy started licking Marilyn's ear she was cooperating;

1535

Tommy gave Marilyn a hickey on her neck.

Things were getting hot.
Then Tommy slipped his right hand under her blouse then slipped one big Breast

1540 out of her bra.

There was a gawking ugly cowboy that was trying to look at what was going on
between Marilyn and Tommy.

1545 But Tommy kept love strokes with Marilyn's breasts she was breathing hard.
Started sucking her nipples

Tommy got such a big hard on it hurt because he drank too much and had to relive
himself of all the drinks he had and quickly.

1550

Tommy said to Marilyn don't move I'll be right back.

Marilyn was starting to pull her bra back up but tommy stopped her and said
nicely please stay as you are I'll be right back.

1555

When Tommy got up from the table he looked back and Marilyn she was waiting for Tommy her breasts were left out for Tommy. The two peeping toms had their eyes on Marilyn breasts.

A few seconds later:

560 Tommy was finished emptying his bladder then hurried out of the bathroom.

Tommy looked and there were those two-peeping toms were still looking at Marilyn's breasts… she was waiting for me.

565 Tommy was walking to the booth watching that peeping tom thinking they need to mind their own business.

Tommy was only ten feet away from Marilyn when Tommy seen a big wild looking man holding a pistol looking at Marylyn.

Tommy stopped he could tell the wild looking man meant what he was doing and 570 he was jealous as hell he was her x husband standing there watching Marilyn with her breast out and that ugly peeping tom looking down at her open blouse.

The big man with the revolver pointed the gun at the peeping tom and let go with three shots killing him and his friend beside him instantly.

575 Marlin started screaming and saying please to the jealous boyfriend or husband.

(HOLLY SHIT)

Tommy naturally though the wild man would be after Tommy next.

580 Tommy stepped back into the crowd.

Trying to think fast

First thing Tommy thought was thanking god for Mother Nature if I never had to piss that would be me there dead.

85 Then Tommy panicked that wild bastard probably is after me now.

Tommy ran out the side door of the bar from the kitchen to the parking lot and ran to the far end where Tommy's pickup truck was parked.

90 Just before Tommy got to his truck Tommy looked over his shoulder and the wild man with the revolver in his hand was coming straight towards him.

Tommy thought hear he comes;

He is going to kill me Tommy's heart was racing fast.

95 Tommy quickly crawled under another pickup truck next to his.

Tommy was trying to hide. Tommy lying under this truck but could see the wild man walking strait towards him.

The man's boots were three feet from Tommy's head! Tommy was a sitting duck waiting to be plucked. (This was the end)

1600

Tommy was expecting to see the wild man's pistol but instead he opened the door of the truck Tommy was hiding under and started the motor it was his fucking truck Tommy was hiding under.

Fuck the motor started up.

1605 Then it roared he put the truck in gear,

Tommy rolled out from under the wild man's truck and made sure he didn't see Tommy.

Tommy rolled under his truck to safety.

The wild man drove out of the parking lot.

1610 Tommy waited underneath his truck for at least fifteen minutes and Tommy had a few brown spots in his shorts,

Tommy thought of all the trucks in the parking lot why did I half to crawled under the wild man's truck... how could I be so unlucky?

1615 Tommy was so upset he drove back to the ranch immediately the big city was too tough for Tommy;

He was thinking of all the bullshit I was telling her and she played me big time.

I am going to be more careful from now on.

1620 Beautiful Marilyn lied to Tommy about not having a boyfriend she had and x jealous husband she almost got me killed.

That won't happen again.

Dad told me about that kind of woman.

1625 Marilyn was coning me and Tommy was playing right into it by telling her that bull shit story about his dying wife. I never had a wife.

She had me all the way innocent bull shit-and I wonder what plan she had for the heartbroken country bumpkin... this will never happen again.

1630 Thanks for the warning pops

CHAPTER -8
TOMMY FIRST SUCSESFULL CON

635

Everyone teachers and friends said in school always told Tommy he was the fastest sprinter they ever seen.

Playing baseball very rarely would the catcher throughout Tommy steeling a base

640 he was to fast or the catcher was to slow tommy would steel all three bases most of the time.
But only for fifty yards)

He could stretch it out to seventy-five yards'
645 If the Appointee wasn't that fast
In track and field, the coach clocked Tommy at world record time at a distance fifty yards in 3:7 seconds the coach was amazed at that kind of speed.

The coach made Tommy run over and over trying to make the two stop watches
550 say something different.
The coach said Tommy your setting world track records every time you run!

No one ever came close to beating Tommy at fifty yards in school.

555 The coach then took Tommy to the Calgary University told the track and field coach to see if Tommy could really run like his stop watch was telling him.

The track and field coach said we'll soon find out.
The city coach called four of the university champions their fastest sprinters.
560

The coach told the university champs here is one the southern Alberta's fastest sprinters pointing at tommy.
Let's see if he can run that fast here.
Everyone lined up it was a one-hundred-yard dash.
65

Further than Tommy wanted to run.
The city coach shot his pistol the race was on;

Tommy ran away from the university athletics easy the first part of the race
70 opened up six feet lead or more.

Tommy held the lead to around eighty yards.

Then two long legged runners just nosed Tommy out at the end.

1675

Tommy finished third out of four runners only was beaten by a few inches.

The university coach told the high school coach all he needs is train more.
He can run especially at the start exceptional.

1680 (Then summer brake was starting and Tommy had to work on the ranch.)

Tommy quit school and never tried to have a foot racing carrier.
Tommy was needed on the ranch.

1685

THREE YEARS LATER

The set up at the whole in the wall hide out in the desert away from everywhere.

1690

The little cattle camp for the old cowboys an outlaw hideout at the old empress
hotel in the Bad Lands south east of brooks Alberta Canada

695   Tommy was seriously becoming a con man.

Tommy played the con with all his friends but was not serious until now.

700   Tommy was well known in the snooker tour in Alberta after beating the champ of them all father Bill marks no one would play Tommy for money.
(If they know who he was)

Tommy had a group of hustlers he hung out with didn't trust any of them.

705   Tommy was thinking of a way to trick people to bet against Tommy sprinting fifty yards.
Tommy dressed like an over wait man wore work boots.

Stuck Kleenex in his cheeks making him look fat and talk slow
710

Tommy went to see the soft ball tournaments held every week end in all the little towns in Alberta and Saskatchewan and British Columbia.

They were all athletes walked around with track shorts and runners on.
715   Tommy thought it looked like a berry patch to make some cash.

Dads said always take the edge (no one knows TOMMY COULD RUN)

Tommy always carry s extra wait.
720   It didn't look like Tommy was a sprinter or could run at all.

Tommy thought it would be better if someone else did the talking meaning the set up!
And there was one aggravating big mouth guy called Fast eddy church he could
725   get a rise out of the pope the most aggravating man on earth just a few words and everyone would take offence.

If Tommy could make a deal with eddy to handle the setup of for the cash, make the bêtes insults everyone all at the same time.
730

Fast eddy found it natural.
Fast eddy had to run for his life several times.

Just what tommy needed?

1735

Tommy would certainly out run anyone at a distance of fifty yards.

Mr. Fast eddy church' main con was selling Grave stones and coffins he had a way of making the grieving family paying top price and more for his Grave stones
1740 making them feel bad if they were cheap.

Eddy church was a good talker or hustler they say Mr. Church had the gift of the gab and more.
Church was not his last name but it made everyone trust the crook.
1745

Tommy knows his name it was Fast eddy on his card.
But he name was Lascaux eddy was a yucky fast eddy never used that name ever.

Tommy called fast Eddy for a meeting.
1750 Told eddy the deal of setting up everyone in a crowd getting everyone's money tommy asks can you perform eddy?

Tommy asked can you handle that Eddy?

1755 Just what's my cut? Fast eddy was interested.

Tommy said on the empress con you have to play this different then the soft ball.

First, you have to play then sad Eddy church grave stone and comfortable coffins
1760 salesman having a few too many drinks to forget the last burial.
The funeral upset you so much, that's how you start the set-up Eddy.

Get everyone to trust you and insult them at the same time then we'll have their cash before they even know what hit them Tommy said, make them feel sorry for
1765 you first, then make them angry, that works every time.

Tommy said eddy can you handle that?
Eddy said yes, the split is fifty/ fifty.

1770 Tommy said I am putting up the cash and there's a chance that someone out runs me from time to time.

So, I'll give you thirty per cent.
I'll take seventy that means thirty to you.
Eddy you have nothing to lose just runs your mouth.

775

Fast eddy s was thinking for a while then said let's do it.

Tommy said one more thing Eddy you try to find the hot spots to pull the con.

780 OK fast Eddy said I'll start looking tomorrow.

I'll call the ranch the night before the set up and you can stop eating, tuck up get ready tommy fast eddy was in.

785 Tommy said don't worry I'll be ready.

Eddy said there are (lots of want to bees) out there that think there fast.
I'll find some good places.

790 In three days- Fast Eddy called and told Tommy of an old hotel south of Brooks twenty miles it's a small spot called Empress Alberta.
It was an old cattle camp.

Tommy, it a place like no other full of Hill Bellies and it's a hide out because
795 Empress is a whole in the wall every criminal in the territory hides out there until the heat is off, the gangsters have money and they like to gamble.

Eddy said let's go get their cash Tommy.

800 OK Tommy said I'll come pick you up at four tomorrow, we'll rehearse the con on the way over there.

It's about one-hour drive from Lightbridge to empress east to the Bad Lands desert.
805

Eddy said bring lots of cash I have it all worked out you better be able to run fast eddy said.
Tommy then said let me worry about the cash and the running eddy.

810 The next morning Tommy slept almost tell 12 noon then had a cold shower

Tommy only had coffee.
It was one hour the Lethbridge.

1815   Just before Tommy got to fast eddy's grave stones store

Tommy wondered how can fast eddy sleep with a bunch of grave stones and coffins.

1820   Tommy said man I couldn't do that.
But it never bothered eddy one bit.

Tommy knocked on eddy's door two thirty and he was still in bed.

1825   Eddy came out with a blanket around him and told Tommy to come back in one hour.
Well Tommy things fast eddy had a girl in the sack and was not finished yet.

Then Tommy went down and got a seven up.
1830
Waited for two hours then drove back to fast eddy's old store. That place made Tommy sick every time he looked in the window there was a coffin for sale and grave stones.
And eddy was still drunk.
1835   Eddy was saying let's go fat boy ha.

We'll talk on the way up to the whole in the wall bar the empress hotel.
OK Tommy said, get sharp eddy.

1840   Make sure you get every one of those crook's dollars get all the bets,
Write all bets down and their names down.

Eddy said I'll get that and then we know who we have to pay.

1845   Tommy told eddy to get a scribbler out of the glove box it will fit in suit pocket.

We pulled into the small hamlet and just in case anything went wrong we parked up the street away from the old hotel.

850

Eddy went in first passed his Grave stone and coffins business cards around.

The cards had an innocent eddy church on the card.

855 Then eddy said to all the outlaws in the bar I just lost my mother,
And had a sad look
 The outlaws had a good heart and sent him a few beers.

Then Tommy walked in and set in the opposite side wall of the shabby hotel.
860

Tommy and Fast eddy made out they never know each other.

One outlaw asks who is your partner sensing we know each other.

865 Eddy said he delivers the grave stones and coffins for me. Eddy was sharp setting
the stage I was his flunky.

But he can't sit with me he works for me.
The set up was on;
870

They thought Tommy and eddy were two dumb flunkies (SQUARE JOHNS)

Fast eddy then said what do you people do for excitement away out here and
smirked,
875 Trying to get under the outlaw's skin and boy it worked.
 eddy had an arrogant style that could irritate anyone.
 Fast eddy started by going table to table with the quarter game and lost two or
three dollars at each table.

880 The one outlaw said it seams you have a gambling problem Mr. church.

Then eddy smiled and said I will bet on anything it's my way of life

 There's a fly on old fat Tommy I'll bet you the fly will go to the direction of the
885 bar.

Any takers five bucks.
Yep one of the outlaws took eddy's bet.

1890   In a minute, the fly went towards the door. Eddy lost again.

Then drank his beer

Eddy then said fuck you assholes.
1895
I'll even bet my fat Dumas's driver can out run anyone here for fifty yards he's too fat to run any further any takers,

Tommy said "please eddy I haven't run since I was in grade school.
1900
Eddy said, oh that's all right there's no one here can run either.

Then the leader outlaw said I'll bet you one hundred big ones, there is old fleet foot setting right next to you he can run.
1905
Out in the crow's nest pass carrying two cases of beer and the night money bag.

Eddy then said OK I will gamble on anything but my fat man needs odds,

1910   I'll put up five hundred dollars to your thousand and you're on as eddy took another drink.

The outlaw said it's a bet but we will only put up twenty-five hundred to your one thousand.
1915   Eddy jumped up and said give the bartender the money and I will give him mine.

Then out the front door of the old rickety hotel all the Gangsters followed and eddy was watching for their move.

1920   Eddy knows they all wanted in on cleaning out a stupid grave stone coffin salesman.

Eddy Winked at Tommy, hold off walk around, give fast eddy time to work all of them I'll try and get more bets, Tommy winked back.
1925
Tommy was telling eddy he can't run that's too much money the gangsters heard tommy saying that.

Eddy please I am out of this (Tommy was saying)

930   Just then Eddy shouted at Tommy dam you.

You work for me and I pay you you're fucking still working so shut up.

Eddy made it look good.

935

One slender looking young man started warming up and he looked like he could run.
Tommy was wearing gum boots and bib overalls and was standing there pushing his stomach out.

940

It looked bad for old drunken eddy and the fat delivery driver.

All the rest of the crooks hiding at empress had seen a chance to take advantage of old drunken square Eddy church they were smiling how easy is this.

945

There were twenty outlaws wanting to bet poor eddy
Eddy played it perfect and said how much you want to bet.

The crowd of crooks counted all their cash.
950   It came to five thousand dollars.

Eddy said to fuck your assholes want to take all my expense money.

If I lost that it would put me out of business.

55

The crooks started saying eddy you're scared.

Your big mouth got you into trouble, hasn't it?
The leader said to eddy.

60

That's when they knew they had big mouth Eddy church.

Eddy said to Tommy go see how much cash is under the seat of the truck knowing Tommy had the cash all the time.

65

But Tommy walked over to the truck and pretended to get eddy's cash.

Fast eddy counted his cash it came to three thousand dollars.

1970   Eddy said OK three thousand of my cash to five thousand of yours.

They took it thinking it was a cinch.

Eddy said to the empress hotel owner you have to hold the cash,
1975   he agreed.

Just before they lined up at the starting line eddy told Tommy this guy can run
Tommy.
If you can don't beat him but only a few inches' tommy, said I'll play it close.
1980

The starter was ready the crooks were smiling at fat Tommy and licking their
chops this was easy money they thought.

1985   Tommy pulled the bib overalls up ready to run and still had the gum boots on.

The gun sounded and off they went.

Tommy had two feet on the outlaw,
1990   Tommy looked over his shoulder and eased off just a little making it look like the
outlaw was going to catch and beat Tommy.

Tommy played it smart won by one foot only.

1995   But the crook said I would have beaten that fat bustards I got a bad start.
That's the only way the fat ass beat me he shouted.

Then eddy collected the cash and said yes you would have beaten the fat guy.
But you fucked up on your start Thanks' eddy said.
2000

Then the boss of the outlaws came out and said Ok I'll put up the cash how much
cash do you have eddy.

Eddy said I don't think I want to gamble anymore.
2005   That angered them more!

The outlaw boss said one more time you put up your eight thousand Eddy.
 To my ten thousand

010 Eddy agreed but made out like he didn't want to gamble on it.

The cash was up.
They were at the starting line.

015 Tommy taking off the bib overalls and the gum boots

 Ready for the pistol to sound
Bang, it went off the race was on Tommy opened up at least ten feet wining easy.

020 The outlaws all lost their money they were cleaned out of every dollar they had.

 Eddy and Tommy grabbed the cash from the hotel owner and ran to their old
pickup truck and spun the wheel out of there before they even had a chance to
think.
025 I am sure they figured it out shortly after we left.
 But it was too late they have been had.

Then came the big fight between fast eddy and Tommy
 Eddy had the cash in his pocket. And saying fifty/ fifty Tommy
030 Tommy drove away from empress got out of their reach.

Then tommy seen an old road and pulled over and grabbed eddy by his hair.

Then said we made a deal you get twenty-five per cent now.
035

 Mr. Eddy you're going to be good with your word,
 eddy said with a snooty voice?
Tommy then pushed eddy out of the truck and was about to physically take the
money and leave eddy beaten in the side ditch.
40

Eddy knows he was no match against Tommy.

 Then Eddy gave Tommy the cash or would get beat up and lose the money
anyway.

2045

Then Eddy counted his twenty-five per cent and it was a lot of money for doing nothing but running his mouth for two hours for $4500.00.

Then Tommy and Eddy were ok but Eddy tried.

2050   Had to watch that fleabag all the time could never trust fast eddy.

Before Tommy arrived back to eddy's grave stone store Eddy asked Tommy did you beat that guy easy or did he make you run hard Tommy;

2055   Then Tommy looked at Eddy and said that was the easiest fourteen thousand we ever made, he never even tested me didn't you see the race. No eddy said, I won by ten feet and was walking. Eddy answered I was watching the money!

I had to pull myself the whole way through he was the slowest.
2060   I had no problems beating them at all.

Then Eddy said I will find another con ok Tommy next weekend let's do it.

Tommy said I will put up the cash and you can take 30% this time now Tommy
2065   said do I have to watch you?

Because if I do I'll be fucking angrier next time

Then Eddy said I'll try and find a faster Appendant I would like to see you get beat
2070   Tommy.
Eddy said with a lot of sarcasm you're a fucking arrogant bustard and cheap/

Tommy looked and said just do your fucking job we are not friends.
Tommy looked fast eddy with bad eyes then warned eddy.
2075

If I were you Mr. Fast eddy church, I would keep my fucking big mouth shut and keep honest.
(Don't give me a reason to fuck you up) Fast Eddy knows tommy would come after him if he had too.
2080   This was Tommy's first successful con and the first time Eddy and Tommy tried it.

Tommy then told eddy we have a good con it works Eddy we have to get along.

We will travel to all those small-town sports days you line it up. No more hotels.
085

Eddy said I will have something as fast as I can I'll call you shortly get ready you
might run into a runner.

Tommy answered eddy, Dad told me always takes the edge and yes there will be
090 hard races.
But eddy I'll trick them if there hard to beat.

Eddy you haven't seen nothing yet.

095 This is easy money, nobody gets hurt and everyone thinks their runners anyway.

Tommy told eddy there's more people want to bet there watching but you never
say anything to them we should have cleaned the whole town out.

100 Eddy you're not getting everyone.

Tommy said you're missing too many people.
I might have to get somebody else.
Eddy said I'll get every dollar that's there.
105

OK Tommy said, 30% to you and Eddy if I catch you cheating me it won't be nice.
Eddy do you hear me?

Tommy said and looked at Eddy.
10 Eddy said there won't be any cheating and fuck you Tommy.

Tommy said call me or I'll call you if something good comes up.

Three day later Dad called Tommy in to talk.
15

Dad asked what's the matter can't you shoot snooker anymore.
Tommy answered no I never quit but no one will play for anything anymore.

Dad laughs and said the gag is out ha you're finished around here. You will learn
20 you should keep moving even before they figure it out.
You should be half way out of town.

I must find another way to make a buck Tommy told his father.

2125 Old bill looked at Tommy and asked is that why you and fast Eddy cleaned out all those crooks that were hiding over at the old empress hotel.

Tommy said I thought it was a good con.

2130 Old bill told Tommy that's a good way to disappear,
Get killed son.
Don't fool with those guys'.

I Hear you and Fast Eddy took all they had between all of them and their mad as
2135 hell.
They figured it out.
Old bill told Tommy you take two thousand cash back so they can start over.

I will call right now and tell them you're coming today.
2140

Tommy said OK I'll drive over there now.

Dad picked up the phone and called empress Hotel.

2145 Tommy could heir old bill laughing and telling the guy on the phone to be more careful from now on!
Tommy said to dad how you know those crooks.

Dad said oh we use to be friends back in the day.
2150

And Tommy how did you con those cons' they are some of the beast cons I ever seen it's almost impossible to con them.

You must have tricked them good.
2155

Fast Eddy and you tommy have coned some of the smart con man in this country.
And that's amazing! But don't do that again.
They have similar cons.

2160 Dads then said Tommy don't con small people, stay away from those hotels.

Then mom said you conned those guys out of there last fourteen thousand dollars;

They haven't got anything to start over.

165

Now Tommy Dad shook his head and said you and fast eddy hit five other small town bars cleaning the poor people out of all their drinking money. The hotel owners are mad you're taking their money.

170   Tommy stops that.   (Dad was serious)

The hotel will have to shut down if you continually taking all their drinking money. Then Dad said me and your mother will help the other five towns.

175   But don't do that you're coning the wrong people.
Go over and give those old friends of ours two thousand dollars back and then get ready to Con the hell out of Calgary's finest city cops.
Your mother and I will tell you about it when you get back from CHAPTER 10-THE cop's, as soon as they put on those uniforms their heads get big.
180   They think they're better in every way then a normal citizen.
They think they are the best.
Tommy gets that kind.
Not the small people you have to have class.

185   Leave the working people along even try and help them and Tommy one more thing when you clean out a hustler never leave him broke.

Give him startup money that s the difference between a class hustler and an ass whole.
90   Remember that, Dad and mom gave Tommy a concerned look.
Then mom said Tommy you be a class hustler don't hustle just go after other hustlers! If you can't do that just stop?

Dad telling tommy where to go for a big con
95

Then Dad told Tommy there's a good spot for a big hustle Tommy in three days there's a Calgary city police are having a yearly sports day at southeast Calgary at Ryerson Park.
They have a slow pitch soft ball tournament and track and field.
00   You get Fast Eddy and take every dollar they have. Slow those cops attitude down.

(Don't tell them your name ;)
Play country bumpkin war

here your old field straw hat.
2205 Another thing Tommy gets real sharp there's some fast cops there catching thieves every day and they train all the time their fit.

OK Tommy said I'll tell Eddy about having different names and we are going up to see if the Calgary police can run.
2210 Dads told Tommy take them; for everything you can.
Yes, Sir Tommy answered. That sounded like and order.

I'll drive over to empress give them two thousand back, then to Lethbridge and tell Eddy about Calgary.
2215 Then get back to the ranch and get ready to really run.

Dad told Tommy you could get a pile of cash there take at least ten thousand with you to bet.
Get them hard! Cause as muck havoc as possible!
2220 Dad said Tommy the cops think there all athletes,
There vulnerable.
Tommy said I will have fast eddy at his top form he will con every one of them if Eddy see money he doesn't care who's it is eddy will go after it, and Fast eddy church is the most aggravating son of a bitch I ever seen.
2225
Old Bill said Tommy he will do the same to you?
Tommy said I know it Dad?
I have to watch Fast Eddy the cops and out run every one of them besides?

2230 DAD SAID-FIRST TOMMY YOU DRIVE BACK TO EMPRESS AND GIVE THE OLD HUSLTERS TWO THOUSAND DOLLAR START UP MONEY BACK YOU BROCK THEM:
Tommy agreed right now.

2235 Then Tommy drove into the old rundown town of empress walk into the old bar and there the not too successful gang was.
They were sitting at a table with not one beer glass on their table looking sad, tommy smiled.
They looked at Tommy as he walked in. Not a word was said'

Tommy said Dad told me to give you gentleman back some startup money
That's why I am here.

Then the boss said thanks Mr. Tommy.
245 If we would have known, you were Billy marks son.
We would not have bet you one cent.
I guess you're going to carry Billy's torch your father was the best hustler we ever
seen now the apple don't fell to far from the tree.

250 But you're showing your fathers class.

Thanks Tommy for the two thousand and your even better than your Daddy you
fooled us and we don't get fooled easy.

255 Please give the best regards to young Billy.
" Tommy said yes Sir Tommy said on his way to the door.
The bosses stood up and said if you ever need anything don't hesitate to ask.
Tommy said thanks and the best to all of you.

260

CHAPTER 11-

Then Tommy drove to Lethbridge to see Fast Eddy.

265 Drove up in front of the window with a coffin and grave stone on display

That turned Tommy off.
Tommy hated coming there.
Rang the doorbell and there was Eddy with very little cloths on drinking with
270 another lady.

"Eddy said come in Mr. Eddy had his measuring tape saying have a sale on
Pick out one that fits you Tommy. (Comfortable coffins)

2275   Then smiled and tipped the beer he was drinking.
   Meaning one of his comfortable coffins
  When the beer was finished Eddy said what's up

   You never come and visit unless you're up to something.
2280

  Tommy got serious" and told Eddy we have a big one coming up in two days.
  Eddy said OK tells me.
  Tommy told Eddy we are going after the Calgary city police.

2285   Eddy said are you fucking crazy. The whole police force is you mark?
  EDDY THEN THOUGHT FOR A FEW SECONDS IT MIGHT WORK.

  Eddy then said them fuckers chase me occasionally let's fuck them good Tommy.

2290   Tommy said be ready Saturday at seven in the morning Eddy you fucking be ready
  it's a big hustle.
  I am bringing $10.000 cash just to start the con if we lose that it's over.

   Eddy looking surprised (TEN thousand to start the betting)
2295

   Tommy told Eddy be very professional
   I am playing a fat hair lip farm boy warring bib overalls and work boots.
  You can go with the same grave stone salesman down on your luck show that
  heartbreaking card with that innocent face on it (Edward church) why don't you
2300   use your own name! Eddy said nobody would trust me using Last chuck.

   You get to everyone that always works with that innocent look

   Eddy had a small note pad to keep track of who's betting what.
2305   Eddy you better sharp because those cops will be questioning you.
  There the sharpest people to run a con on they have seen everything almost.

  Don't tell them anything say we were just drinking under a tree watching the
  sports day and I thought it would be OK to try and see if the fat farm boy could
2310   run like he said he could.
   And Eddy stay sober and fucking sharp this is dangerous.
   Eddy said I'll be sober and ready we'll clean those dead heads out.
   Then Tommy told Eddy get the whole crowd not just a few. The whole Fucking

Park of them!

315   **Yes, Eddy said I realize this is serious, I'll do my best.**

    Tommy told Eddy I will see you in thirty-six hours.

    And walked out of that morgue of a house Eddy lived in

320

    Tommy hated going in there.

It was a sunny Saturday morning Eddy and Tommy pulled into the parking lot at Ryerson park in south east Calgary.

325   As we were parking Tommy's truck Eddy asked Tommy to do you think we should do this.

Tommy said why not fuck the cops.
Eddy said please park our get way truck out on the street then.

330

Tommy then said good thinking and turned the truck to a street curve outside the park.
Then eddy said OK let's get it on as he opened his door. Let's set under that big tree portend we are drinking a beer I brought a six pack of empties tommy said smiling.

335   **Eddy told Tommy put some sponge in your mouth and those old shit stained work boats on and wait under that tree over there acting dumb like you usually do.**

    Then Eddy told Tommy give me the ten thousand cash.

340   **Tommy said Eddy get them all think every time you open your mouth these are trained cop's it's a weird hustle.**

    Don't worry Tommy.
    Let's get out of heir before they figure it out.

345   **Tommy said I am putting in the sponge and my old glasses on.**
    And putting on yellow cake coloring on my teeth I am a hillbilly?

THE SET UP
    Tommy watched the whole lame thing.

350

    There were cops with white running shoes and racing shorts.

They looked the part of athletes.
Showing off to their girlfriends and wives and anyone Elis that was looking
2355 running around like cock roosters.
Eddy started conversations with them.

They told Eddy they had gold medals for track and field from university and high
school.
2360 Fast Eddy was starting to con asking how the elite police officers trained and what
dangers they were in and even saying that he was proud of them.

Every one of them had a near death defying story for stupid Eddy.

2365 Eddy stood there playing like he was amazed.

They were all heroes.
Eddy almost had their trust now.

2370 The police thought Eddy was a stupid working stiff.
Then eddy showed his ancient looking card.

It wouldn't take long now.
Tommy was watching the set up and fast Eddy was playing on their egos and they
2375 all had big ones.
Eddy was making then heroes. Saying he must clean up after them.
Tommy was anxious to run them but was thinking he might run into a runner.

Tommy listing to the conversations it was unbelievable ego
2380 Come on eddy Tommy was ready.

It was taking Eddy a long time.
Then Eddy looked at the cop with the biggest ego of all and said my fat country boy
said he can run some.
2385

Eddy then said I don't know him we just met a few minutes ago but I am a
gambler Eddy said goading the cop with a smart alike style.
Only fast Eddy could do.
Then Eddy said:" I'll bet you one hundred dollars for your two hundred.
2390 I am taking a big chance so I need two to one odds.

That fat boy I just met he is just a simple sort.

Eddy said he is a little fat and out of shape.

395

I don't think he can run go farther than fifty yards.

Would you give him a chance sir and make yourself an easy hundred at the same time!

400   The hero officer looked at the fat farmer with work boots and bib overalls,"

And said well if he wants to run ask him first the cop said I don't want to take advantage of him eddy said it's my hundred not his so you're not taking advantage of him.

405

The set up was on;
Tommy agreed to only run one time!

The cop ran over to a crowd of cops and their girlfriends and he told them.

410

I can buy the beer now because there are the stupidest country bumpkins I ever seen over under that tree and they want to match me of all people to run a sprint of fifty yards.
That's right down my alley.

415   I am a sprinter the cop said.
The whole crowed looked at Eddy and the fat bumpy bib overalls old wore out straw hat fat farm boy and laughter all over the park.

The cop gave Eddy his two hundred.

420   Went to the track had white running shoes and track shorts he looked like he would destroy the fat farmer.
Tommy stood at the starting line bib overalls and warring work boots.

Everyone was looking at a real country bumpkin.

25

Then the other cops thought they might get some of this easy money.

They yelled at Eddy and said you got any more money to lose. Eddy said some.

30   Then the cop's friends lined up to get there bet in before this stupid Eddy guy ran

out of money and their wives.
 Eddy took the righting pad out of his pocket

Tommy and fast Eddy were working the cops like they were school children.

2435

All of Ryerson park cops and their friends lined of to bet on their finest.

It took around thirty-minute Eddy had a note book out keeping track of who bet.

2440 Then the police organized a starter and two judges at the finish line.
All smiling acing like they were good sports.

 Tommy walked by Eddy and asked is it all on.
 Eddy said every cent and two thousand more than the cash we have.
2445 Tommy and eddy both winked at each other? Twelve thousand dollars what if we lose, eddy said meat you at the getaway truck.

They were about ready to run.
All the cops and their wives and girlfriends were smiling this was a big joke.

2450

They all were saying we should give them back some of the money.

They don't know what they're getting into.

2455 # The race
The starter had a pistol and said when you heir the shot the race starts.
Tommy ran with work boots and bib overalls.
 The cop gave Tommy a look of poor little country boy as they lined up for the start.
2460

This was for $12.000.00 dollars Tommy was going to run hard.
 Bang the pistol sounded.

They were neck and neck side by side half way down they were tied.

2465

Then Tommy had another gear and opened up five feet to win easy winner.
Running with work boots and bib overalls on

Then Eddy had the cop's money.
470

You could see the mood change.

And then the chief took over and started investigating.

475   Fast Eddy he took Tommy name then called our names in and found out there was
charges.
No charges.
Then there was a cop athlete. The cops wanted to match their special fast cop.
Eddy said how much money.
480   They lined up and eddy took forty thousand dollars' worth.
But negotiated two to one eddy put up twenty thousand to their forty.

THE SECOND RACE FOR FORTY THOUSAND
Tommy took off the work boots and the bib overalls then spit out the sponge that
485   was in his cheeks.
Tommy was going to run in bear feet.
The cop was ready for the start tommy and the top cop lined up the gun shot.
Tommy was off before the gun went off just a split second but opened up two
lengths halfway down the track the con pulled up beside tommy they eye balled
490   each other than the last tommy found another stride and won by a full foot.
Eddy had all the money and was jumping up and down.

Tommy felt the work boots and bib rove roles.
Tommy looked at eddy and said do you have the cash all of it eddy answered yes.
495   Then tommy and eddy made their exit running as fast as they could to the truck
and drove away.

Then one of their junior police officers that went to school with Tommy and told
the chief that that's Fast Eddy church and Tommy marks.
00

Nobody can out run Tommy ever he is the fastest in the world at fifty yards.
Then the chief said why you didn't tell us.

Well I never recognized Tommy until he was about to start the last race when he
05   spits that sponge out of his cheeks.

You were all set up; fast Eddy church is one of the smoothest talkers in the country along with Tommy Marks Donily.

2510 Sir that's a deadly commendation

Tommy" Handle is the cowboy con man.

Eddy in called Fast Eddy church.
2515

Then the chief said they came heir to fuck us we have been had.

The cop that lost the race said arrest them both.

2520 The chief said that would make the Calgary police force look like stupidest cops in the country. But we will get them somehow.

Eddy was excited we just won $40.000.00 clear.
By this time there were reporters that witnessed the Calgary cities finest being
2525 coned out of fort thousand cash and the two slick hustlers that did it?

Fast Eddy church and Tommy ran to their pickup truck.

There were cop cars everywhere we couldn't even drive out of the parking lot.
2530

Most streets were blocked there was something big happening.

Tommy said let leave the truck here then Tommy and Eddy walked a few blocks to the shamrock hotel.
2535 And set at a table and ordered two Canadian beers.

We relaxed Eddy counted the money and never tried to cheat Tommy.
Then gave Tommy his ten thousand betting money back
Then took 20% of the thirty thousand we just coned out of the cops.
2540

It was the best con we pulled yet we enjoyed the evening laughing lots of drinks.

Then we stayed for the night in the old shamrock hotel.

2545 Eddy kept coming over to Tommy's room checking to see if Tommy was still there.

Tommy asked what the matter

Eddy said there's something real big going on those cops are running around everywhere I hope there not after us

550

Tommy said no Eddy those cops could have arrested us anytime there after someone ells. Go to sleep Eddy.

The next morning, we were eating bacon and eggs and thinks were starting to get
555 back to normal.

Then the china men in the restaurant showed us the newspaper.

The Chinese man pointed to the pictures in the paper and asked "Is this your gentleman.
560 The china man said asked are you the cowboy con man and fast Eddy church two well know hustlers.

One of the cops said this combination spells disaster.

565 There was a big head line (two con man fleas the city copses out of at least $40.000 dollars.

The two-con man teamed up were (Fast Eddy Church) and the (Cowboy Con man) Tommy Marks Donily.

Soon as Tommy seen that Tommy said let's get out of here fast. They walked back
570 to the truck and were on the way out of Calgary.

They both went home.

And stayed there for some time before people would forget about that con especially the cops?
575 At home one thing mom said to Tommy you did a good job Tommy you created a lot of trouble for the city cops.

They hated you guys so bad you took most of them away from the jobs.

There were two of you cousins from the state's New York that are very grateful to
80 you.

Tommy asked why

Then mom said your cousins were in jail and had very serious charges.

The cops had evidence on them they were going to get at least ten years.
85 There were two kilos of cocaine and two pistols all locked up in the evidence room

just waiting for their trial to present it as evidence and without that evinces they will be realest shortly.

While you were pulling your com, someone was lowered down the ventilation pipe
2590 and removed all the evidence on them.
Now they will be free.
They have no evidence to convict them they were going to get ten years or more.

Tommy said there were other things going on mom.
2595

Yes, Tommy there were two other cousins of your that dropped steel tire spikes punctures trucks cars under all under pass's in down town Calgary.

That drove the cop's crazy there were car pile ups all over town.
2600

Your family in New York will not forget you.
Tommy, you just did them one hell of a favor.

Then mom said Tommy you give us that forty thousand you made.
2605

We are putting that in a savings account for your old age which might be sooner than you think the way you're going.
OK Tommy then gave mom the cash.

2610

2615

2620

FUCK THE COPS- says the- COWBOY CON MAN & FAST EDDY CHURCH!!
Cowboy Way's

CHAPTER 12

Tommy stays home on the ranch for the rest of the summer working on the ranch now putting up winter feed for the cows.

2645　**Tommy stopped all cons until the heat was off people forgotten fast.**

It was late in the fall September and it was haying time Leonard and Tommy were putting up the winter feed for over one thousand head of cows the 7H ranch.

2650　We had to hand load and stake one hundred thousand.
Eighty-pound bales of hay for the winter.
It was hard work but we were almost finished after we stacked the winter feed.

Brother Leonard and Tommy had a plan to go to Spokane Washington and claim a race
2655　horse or maybe two.

It was close to winter and racing was about to be shut down for the winter,
And the race horses were running for at least half of what they were worth.
We were going to take advantage of that.
2660　So we were in a big hurry to finish and get to Spokane Washington.
The last load was complete.

Leonard and Tommy were extremely fit after all that lifting and work on the farm and ranch.
2665　The family was all horse trainers dating back to Ireland & England three generations.

We were the third-generation horse trainers and we all were very handy with a horse!
Leonard went to Dad and told him everything was finished and we were going to claim some fast horse's in Spokane Washington at the race track called play fair race course.
2670

Leonard came back and told Tommy to load up that old plug horse you have and go to Spokane, and run him one time then we will be illegible to start claiming horse's.

That was the tract rules you had to race a horse before you and claim a horse (eligibility)
2675　Then Leonard told Tommy load old caribou red up and goes to Spokane and race old red.

Then call me and I will come and then we will claim a couple horses.

Tommy watched for good claims.

680 OK Tommy was excited the next morning Tommy was loading everything and Leonard gave Tommy two hundred dollars.

Tommy said that's not much, but Leonard said I'll be there shortly make it last.

685 Tommy said he would look after it. Leonard said I'll be there in a few days.

Tommy loaded caribou red in the horse trailer and headed south to Spokane Washington.

690 Tommy only had $200 dollars to survive on but Leonard said he would be there in a few days.

Leonard said I'll gather up some cash and come down later.

Tommy, you study those horses let's get some good ones.

695 Leonard said after they run follow them back to their barn make sure their sound. Yes, tommy answered ill know lots in a few days

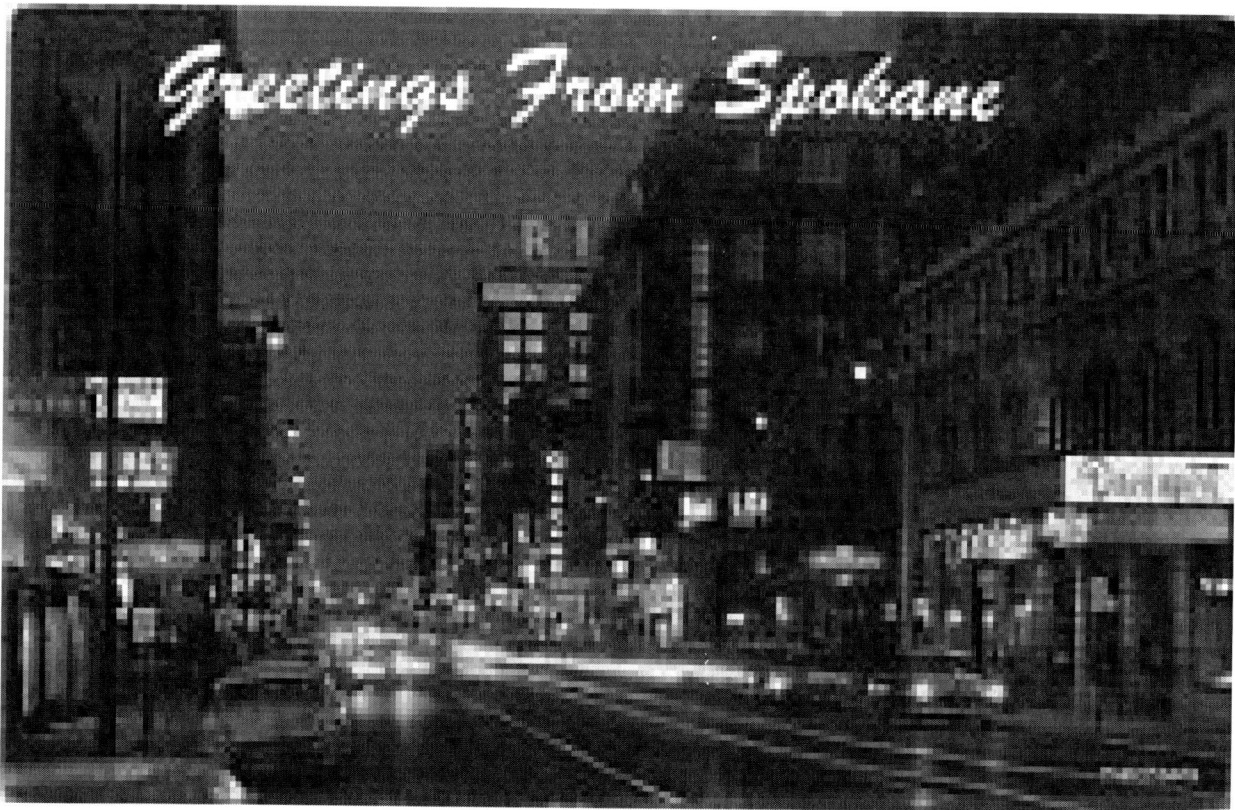

Lots of bar's up and down both sides of Sprague street with a ton's
2700   hungered hustlers

It was the third year Tommy was training horse's Tommy raced around Alberta all summer ended up with a speed horse called caribou red.

2705   Just before Tommy left the ranch to Spokane, Tommy ran into the house and pulled the Diamond Brady pool stick out of his dresser and took a look at it.
The purple sapphires sparkled.
Tommy thought it just might come in handy encase things didn't go right.

2710   Tommy never know he was about to step into the semi big leagues of pool hustlers.

Tommy pulled into play air race course at Spokane Washington.
Unloaded old red right beside a Nabors of ours from Alberta Mr. Hairy Grouch our friend.
2715   Tommy slept in the truck and worked with red trying to get him ready to run and maybe win a few bucks.
Two weeks went by no Leonard.

Tommy borrowed twenty dollars off Mr. Grouch just to eat,
2720   And the truck was cold to sleep in.
So, Tommy made a bed on straw bales with sweaty stinky horse blankets.
In an open stall, next to red

Then another week went by.
2725

Tommy never bathed or eat much Tommy would wait all day for Brother Leonard to show up.
Than when the races started go to the grand stand and have a bag of French fries and gravy the only thing Tommy could afford.
2730

Tommy looked like a bump, never saved or bathed in at least ten days.

Finally, it was three weeks' latter and early one morning brother Leonard walked in with a western suit on with cousin big Louie looking like millionaires.
2735

They seen Tommy standing holding caribou red and walked right by on the way by

Louie said why you don't clean up.

Then Leonard and Louie went straight to Mr. Gooch they started asking him about witch
740   horses to claim,
Didn't care one bit about Tommy

Then asked Mr. Grouch to come and join them at the pan cake house.

745   They were walking to their car Leonard said Tommy go clean up.
  Talk to you when we come back.
Just like Tommy was a hired hand. Tommy waited for around two hours before they
showed up.

50

Play fair race tract Spokane Washington
 Then Leonard told Tommy go get respectable clean up and gave Tommy ten dollars.
Then drove off never came back until the next morning at ten o'clock.

55 Tommy now had to do something to hell with these arrogant bastards.
Tommy knows he was on his own.
Tommy waited for big Louie and Leonard's next move.
Sure, enough the same attitudes.
Leonard and big Louie said Tommy we are going to claim three horse's tonight.

60

 Here's eighty-five hundred dollars' tommy go put that into the racing office account
and get three claim slips.

We will fill them out for tonight races.

2765   Tommy then asked can I take two hundred out for me to buy some clean cloths.

No Leonard said we'll get some tomorrow for you,
Leonard said go put that cash in the office and get ready to claim horse tonight.
Well that just about finished Tommy.
2770   Tommy said to Mr. Grouch Tommy as he walked by would you please look after old
Caribou red for a few days for me.
Then Mr. Grouch smiled and nodded his head seeing how they treated tommy.

CHAPTER 13-

2775   THE BIGGEST TEST FOR TOMMY
Tommy went over to his pickup truck and got a blanket,
 Took it to his stall where he was sleeping.
Leonard yelled Tommy get going;
Tommy said I need to take a piss. Tommy went into an empty stall.
2780

The back walls of the stall were two boards tommy pulled them off they were losing
anyway
Tommy though his hat out on the railway tracks next the Diamond Brady then shimmied
through himself.
2785

 Once out of the race track and onto the railway tracks tommy pulled the stall boards
back together.
Tommy took off away from them and ran down the railway tracks two miles to down
town Spokane sprang street tommy felt free and ran all the way.
2790

 Leaving big Louie and Leonard waiting in front of the barn stall
Tommy smiled wondering how long they waited.
Until they finally look and discover Tommy's was gone man they deeded that.

2795   Fuck them Tommy rented a nice hotel with a Jacuzzi and shower.
Pushes a whole wardrobe of nice cloths then put the new cloth on along with a new
Stetson cowboy hat.
 Then went into a bar and had a beer setting relaxing watching one hustler cleaning out
the whole bar they just about had all the money in the place.
2800   Tommy went to another bar and another,

The whole town was full of pool players.

All the time there was a beautiful red head following Tommy watching what he was doing.

Tommy finally went to his hotel room and sleep for the night but noticed the girl.

805

Tommy had only one thing in his mined his intentions were to see just how good these hustlers are.

Tommy wiped the Diamond Brady it sparkled like magic.

Tommy know he could not use it until the big money comes up it would tip everyone

810 off.

The next day Tommy would start from the bottom playing off the wall.

With and old stick

The morning came Tommy jumped up felt great showered and put his new cloths on and went to all the bars found an old scraped up pool stick in one bar that was Tommy's

815 perfect wait.

Then purses it for six dollars

The queue looked bad no hustler would ever use such a piece of junk.

Then Tommy took the old queue to a queue repair shop and asks the man to implant a

820 hexagon queue on the old stick.

The man laughed and said that's a no-good queue,

Tommy said just how much to install the new tips queue.

825

Well is that all you can afford son. I saw people like you.

You should quick shoot pool putting a good queue on that old stick won't help you that much.

30 Give up that hustling I seen lots just like your son?

Tommy said how much Mr.

Oh, the man felt sorry for the kid then said oh five bucks less than the queue costs.

35 After the man installed the new queue tip,

Tommy asked sir how much that new queue tip cost a normal guy.

Well he said it cost around twenty-five dollars.

2840 Tommy flipped him the twenty-five bucks and said thanks for the new queue tip and
your advice. You might be right.
 The man was surprised, well your one of the ones that has a little money left good luck
kid if you go broke come back I'll loan you a few to get back home!
Tommy said thanks Mr. so tell me who and where these good local hustlers are in
2845 Spokane. The queue repair man told tommy there all over town they go bar to bar
looking for their mark.
 Ok tommy thanked the nice man and walked up the street.

Most of the bars the action was from two bucks to twenty bucks.
2850
 Not that much but.
 Tommy was rusty never played for over six months?

This would be the place to start cut the rust make some small bucks then in eighteen
2855 hours might run into some one with money.
Then the Game's will start.

Tommy started at a small all-night bar they were still drunk from the night before;

2860   The hustlers were sober taking advantages of the drinkers.

Tommy challenged the table where the one hustler was the best in the small bar.

Tommy stared racking the balls.
2865
Then said sir I never played this game for a couple years,

But I guess you want to play for money.
 Yes, the small-time hustler said this table plays for ten bucks,
2870   And put it up before I break the balls.

 Tommy said you city people are always after money.

The hustler broke the balls he scattered them all over the table but none dropped.
2875
Tommy went ahead and ran half the table,

Then played a safety shot.

880 The hustler missed and then Tommy ran the rest and grabbed the twenty dollars from the top pocket.
The bartender started laughing well that's the first game you lost all night to the street hustler. This made him mad.

885 Then the hustler said he just got lucky, hay country boy would you play for $100.00

Then Tommy said Look Mr. you're a lot better player than me.

But I will put up fifty dollars to your hundred, that's two to one, the hustler said rack them cowboy as he through his hundred in the top pocket.
890 Tommy put his fifty dollars in the pocket, the game was on.

The bar tender and all the drunks the hustler just cleaned out were all watching, knowing the young cowboy would get cleaned out because the hustler let most cowboy's win on purpose.
895

Tommy broke and in dropped a red,

Then Tommy ran over half the table then knowing the hustler had a role of money in his pocket.
900 Tommy misted his shot on purpose and played a safety leaving the hustler nothing to shoot.
The hustler shot missing then setting tommy up to run the table.
But Tommy made a few more mistakes and played a miss shot leaving him hocked again.
905 The hustler could not see anything,
It looked like Tommy was just lucky.

Then the hustler shot again and missed, Tommy was set up and ran the table.

10 The hustler was surprised how you can get so fucking lucky.

Everyone said the young cowboy got lucky twice.
One man setting at the bar said hey kid you better run with those bucks you just beat one of Spokane finest he will take everything you have son.
15

Then the hustler said OK cowboy and started counting his cash throwing it on the table he had six hundred.

81

Told Tommy to match it Tommy said no way you're a hustler everyone in the place tells me not to play you for anything.

2920 But I will put up three hundred of my summer wages and match your six hundred.

The hustler said let's do it and started Racking the balls.

Then out of the corner of Tommy's eye there that beautiful red headed lady that
2925 followed him around the day before JUST WALKED IN.

Tommy broke the balls and one red dropped into the side pocket.
Then Tommy ran the whole table and reached into the top corner pocket and pocketed the cash.
2930 The bar was speechless.
The hustler said good shooting cowboy your either lucky or one of the best in Spokane

Tommy said well I get lucky sometimes.
The hustler said well I am broke.
2935 Tommy then slipped forty dollars in his hand, and then gave him a wink.
The hustler's eyes opened wide he knows that move.
He just got hustled then got out of that bar as fast as he could.

The table was Tommy's table but there were no challengers in that little bar.
2940
The red head said hey cowboy you got enough to buy me a drink.
Her name was Judy we had at least six glasses of draft beer, schooners they called them.

Tommy said yes then she ordered another beer.
2945
Tommy asked what a schooner, it was a small glass of draft beer

Judy said come on cowboy I'll take you to some places where they will love to play you for five or six hundred or more! I don't have much to do right now I'll take you all over
2950 to every bar identify every hustler in town.
I know every one of them and the bars to go to.

I don't want any sex or anything ells just buy me a drink and something to eat.

2955 Are you up for it cowboy?

Tommy said maybe Judy I'll try but who you are you a cop.

Judy said cowboy far from it.
960   I just like you style.
Then Out the door and up Sprague Street we went.

Tommy packing that old pool cues with the scraps and even partly shattered.
Judy asked why you are bringing that old stick with you. Tommy never answered.
965

Judy explained the further up Sprague Street we go things get tougher for you cowboy.
But I will tell you who you're challenging.
Tommy said thanks.
Judy told tommy the small hustler you just beat can't make it up on the big Sprague
970   bars.
If you want to step into the lion's den come on cowboy.

Tommy told Judy I am no hustler
I am a country boy that worked all summer hard and just got paid.
975   This is my summer wages.
Judy said well we will soon find out if you can play snooker with the big boys on upper
Sprague.
Judy and Tommy walked through every honky tonk bar on Sprague;
We watched the street sharks and Judy said these guys can really shoot stay away from
980   them Tommy.
Then Judy pointed another two sharks.
Judy said they never play each other stay away from both of them.

"Tommy's thought" he probably has a role of cash in his pocket.
985   I'll go after him later" Tommy said under his breath.
Judy pointed out two of the top sharks and several others that were trying to bees

Tommy was starting to trust Judy and new she was the real McCoy she knew everyone
and everything that happened in Spokane.
990   We were starting to get drunk and it was all most midnight, the whole day and half the
night disappeared so fast.
We naturally were holding hands; we were natural together besides.

The cowboy gently slipped his hand into Judy's pants into her pussy it was small and
995   tight Judy scrammed and then put her arms' around Tommy.

In five minutes Tommy said let's buy something nice to drink like sham pain and go back to my room, Judy said I thought you would never ask. On the way, we stopped at a liquor store and got six bottles on baby duck bubbly chilled.

3000

 In five minutes Tommy handed the room key to Judy to open the room door, Judy slipped the key into the locked door then we entered the room Judy looked around and said this is wonderful Tommy. How can you afford this?

3005 We opened a bottle and the top shot out and hit the sealing,
Then we poured and the bubbles filed the glasses magically then we sipped the refreshing bubbles.
It was nice the atmosphere was a feeling of real friendship.
Then tommy asked Judy let's try that beautiful hot hub with all the underwater colored
3010 light.
Then into the Jacuzzi Tommy hit the bubble Jacuzzi the jets stated. Then we stepped in.
 Tommy reached for judies pussy but Judy had her lags together and stopped Tommy.
Then Judy felt Tommy's huge hard on.
Then Tommy slipped his finger into Judy's pussy, in and out and Judy moaned with
3015 delight.
We both felt like it was right, Judy gently stroked Tommy's pines
Then spread her legs as Tommy mounted her.
Tommy almost blew already but there was no way Tommy was going for the old wham bang thank you ma'am,
3020 Tommy wanted Judy to remember Tommy as one of the best fucks she ever had.

Judy's breasts were hard as a rock now as Tommy licked his tongue over them as he stoked her.
Judy arched her back and purred like a little Kitten. Fuck me Tommy she said hurry
3025 Tommy I can't wait. The strokes went faster and faster then came,
Tommy blow Judy moaned and Judy felt the sperm shoot up into her.
We both made it at the same time.

Tommy felt his cock inside Judy. Judy was a real woman with a strange innocence
3030 about her yet a pro all at the same time.

Judy wanted more and more and she got more?
Even doggie style plus it was the eight times we made love.
We finally went into a contended sleep.

035   Witch Tommy deeded.
The hotel maid woke us up at twelve.
Then we had sex again.
Tommy got up first and ordered coffee.

040   Tommy was starting to think time is running out Leonard and big Louis will be
searching for Tommy probably wanting there eight thousand five hundred buck's backs.

When Judy woke up and had her coffee.
   Tommy said around six or seven tonight in five hours let's go after those five big
045   hustlers you pointed out. Where will they start their night evening hustle?

   Judy said I don't think you can beat any of them.
Judy said I told you to stay away from them that are why I pointed them out so you
could miss them.
050   Tommy said very sharply Judy show me where they start their nightly hustle Judy
shook her head and said OK cowboy.
   I'll take you exactly to your painfully death.
   We will go out to the state line Washington and Idaho state line that's where the money
is it's a meeting place between the two states it's intense.
055   Night clubs on both sides of the boarder.
Tommy ask how far is it out there,
   Judy answered thirty minutes.

We took a cab to Idaho and Washington state boarder to the club closest to us was the
060   biggest.
The Inn on south side it had some of the nicest regulation pool tables around.

Judy pointed out everybody she thought was a player who was standing around the area
by the tables – some of them were very big players Judy said they play the tournaments
065   in Vegas Nevada.
   I told Judy to take me to the weakest table
Judy walked me down the line to the very back of the first bar and told me if you can't
beat this stooge you might as well hang up your cue.
So, I started playing him for twenty bucks
070   Tommy got beat and was trying to win.

We played again Tommy also lost.
Tommy just wasn't ready to play with the big boys yet.

3075   Tommy needed more practice only lost forty dollars.

We left the state line and Judy let me know that it wasn't a great idea Judy felt sorry for the cowboy that thinks he can shoot.

3080   On the way, back to Spokane Judy said Tommy let's just have a good time please stop trying to hustle you're not good enough.

Tommy smiled and said Judy we will enjoy every minute with you.

3085   I am starting small time hustling on Sprague Street.

The night is young.
If you won't stop, I can't help you Tommy Judy said.

3090   Then Tommy told Judy all I need is some practice.
Judy, I worked on the farm hard for the last six months hang in there Judy Tommy will return.

3095   It didn't take much time at the state line;
The night was young the cab stopped on Sprague Street.

Judy and Tommy set at a small table next to the snooker table Judy said there is no state line players in heir now Tommy so get after these bumps.
3100
Tommy put his coin on the table to challenge.
The winner the man said well I played you last night thanks for coming back name your poison Tommy said how about fifty big ones.

3105   The Prague hustler played Tommy play last night and he couldn't get his fifty dollars out of his pocket fast enough.
Thinking it was easy money; Tommy wasn't fooling around this time the games have started for real.

3110

Older Brother Leonard Marks

15

CHAPTER 14-
START OF THE STING
THE A CONFIDENT (COWBOY con man?)

20 Tommy had the brake, and then broke the balls leaving the balls all intact then leaving him nothing to shoot at the far end of the table;
This was different than the state line.
Tommy recklessly broke the balls all over the table leaving his opponent set up everywhere if Tommy would miss.
25 Tommy continued this style of play beating everyone in that bar.
Cleaning them out of over two thousand dollars,

Judy was studded how can shoot like that.
You didn't shoot like that before Tommy.
Tommy replied just getting lucky Judy.

3130

We left that bar and Judy knows of another bar off Sprague.
The word would be out in minutes.
Judy gave the cab driver directions to a truck stop bar.

3135   Then telling Tommy there is a big bar out there with eight nice pool tables.

Tommy said please stop by our room there's something I need.
Tommy ran into the hotel then up to his room then Tommy's Hart skipped a beat when
he picked up Dads snooker champion stick with the purple sapphires the Diamond
3140   Brady.
Tommy needed it mentally and it gave Tommy almost perfect control of the queue ball
like magic.
Tommy gave it to Judy to carry, Tommy carried the old queue.

3145   We were getting out of the cab Judy was studying Tommy's change of attitude.

Judy never said anything but she somehow knew thinks changed with Tommy
somehow had things figured out he was confident and cocky.

3150   Judy didn't know everyone but she pointed out two good players out.

They were both playing on different tables.
That's where Tommy challenges.
Judy said Tommy I just told you to stay away from both of them.
3155

Tommy said its time to get it on darling.

Tommy handily beat the first hustler out of every dollar he had.
Then the second fell the same way.
3160   Judy was amazed.
Tommy cleaned both out of five thousand cash.

Both hustlers wanted away from the cowboy and far away!

3165   Tommy then asked Judy is there another money bar.

Yes, Tommy Judy said let's go.
 After hitting several small bars
 The bartender told Tommy there were two guys just here looking for you and you just missed them.

170 They said you're a hustler that always blow's every dollar and they have to catch you before that happens again.
 And they were fucking mad,
 Especially that big one he was called big Louie!

175 You only missed then ten minutes, there driving all over looking for you.

 They rented an old Volkswagen… you better watch out.

 Judy said I know one bar that the cream Della cream hustlers hang at.
180
 None of the players you played go around there, it's called Girds its and old warehouse fixed up like a palace. It down under the train track overpasses.

 Then Judy said she's never went their ether but I think there away over your head
185 cowboy; let's we better stay away from that lion's den.
 Tommy, you didn't do well out at the state line either tommy this is away tougher then the state line.
 Tommy said let's go see what did you call them the cream Della cream.
 Judy said cowboy that mean's the best!
90
 Judy said ok Cowboy you're going to meet them shortly but this is away harder than the state line even and we know what happen out there!

 Tommy said please take me there.
95 Judy said better go back to the state line,
 No Tommy said.
 Then Judy said let's go then but I think it's a big mistake tommy.
 Tommy like the name a palace called (Girds billiards and bar)

00 Judy was nervous.
 Tommy told Judy look after the queue in that old sack you're carrying I might need it.
 Tommy said with a daring smile.
 Then Tommy said we have to make sure Leonard and big Louis don't catch us.
 The cab stopped in front of Girds bar.

3205   It looked like a class joint Tommy said.

It is Judy told Tommy you will be broke by the time we leave.
Or have a pale full of dollars.

3210   This place… if you beat them they will fly in a big player from Seattle.

You will never leave here with any of their money.

Judy and Tommy entered the palace set at the bar ordered two cold once.
3215   The first table looked like the big boys table.
There were three well-dressed men setting there looking restless.
 The biggest man was shooting trick shots showing off.
Judy asks the friendly bartender who is that trick shooter.

3220   Oh, you don't know him that's Seattle slim.
Slim plays tournaments in Vegas he is the best on the west coast.

 Then Judy said he should be called Seattle fats the man is big
The bartender said I think that's why he's called slim.
3225

There waiting for some stupid sucker small time hustler to come in.

Tommy leaned over and said to Judy keep that queue in that sack don't let anyone see it.
 I will be using it shortly.
3230   Judy's eyes opened wide what's this queue all about.
Tommy said you will see?
Tommy wasn't nervous in fact he was like a hunter, Judy witnessed.

 Tommy asked Judy what you down here on the street tell me Tommy asked
3235   Judy said well I support my mother she is sick,
 So, I sell coke, Mariana I am a small drug dealer that's why I know most everyone at
least on Sprague… I follow the money.
 I have been trying to protect you but I give up now Judy frowned?

3240   Tommy said thanks Judy.
Tommy then said if I go broke give me back a twenty.
Judy said you can't lose all that money.
 Tommy said it's always a possibility Judy eyes opened.

245 To support myself and mom
But one of my users got credit from me and the cops put him in jail.
He will pay but he put me out of business.

Tommy looked for a few seconds.
250 Then asked how much money you need to start again Judy?

Judy answered around seven or eight hundred.
Then Tommy said I'll give you some start up cash before I try these big hustlers.
255 Judy, you helped me Judy thanks.
Tommy then gave Judy $1500.00 dollars and said sweetie put this in your pocket and gives your mother five hundred.
Tommy approached the three well-dressed men

260 In country boy style
Tommy wanted the big man they called him slim… Tommy knew he had the cash.

Tommy said well fats would you play a game I'll bet you ten dollars' sir.

265 The fat man was a little insulted… first kid I am called Seattle slim.
He answered quickly, son you better learn some respect.

And no, you can't play here for ten dollars.

70 And who do you think you are even challenging me.

I only play named or someone who plays for money and that's not ten bucks!

The fat man was looking down at the country boy and his big mouth.
75 My name Seattle slim you little prick.

Slim said I'll fuck play you for five hundred then you can get to fuck out of here and don't bother me again boy.
Tommy answered OK I'll hold my cash and pay you after.
80 No, you put it into the top pocket,
If you don't know that where did you come from?

OK Tommy said as Tommy stuffed his five hundred in the top pocket along with fats or slim.

3285 Then they flipped for the brake Tommy won the flip.

Tommy was still shooting with that old scrapped up queue and fats noticed it and smiled.

Tommy played it smart just ticked off a red not moving a ball then hocking fats on the
3290 far top corner.

Fats got out of the hock without scratching but opened two red balls fats made reckless shot fats under estimated the country boy

Tommy then made three blacks,
3295 Then never took any chance's left fats hocked again.

Fats made another mistake and then Tommy ran most of the table there wasn't enough ball left on the table fats had to start hocking tommy to win.

Fats conceded the game.

Tommy with that stupid country boy shit eating grin pick the one thousand dollars out
3300 of the pocket and folded it and put it in his shirt pocket.

Showing the cash in his shirt pocket that bothered Seattle slim this fucking punk walking around with slim cash in his pocket

Seattle slim was talking to his two partners
3305 They both told slim that he gave the country bun ken so many chances anyone could have beat you.

They said let's clean this big mouth country bum ken out and send him back to the farm.

3310 Seattle slim said cowboy, just how much cash do you have in those jeans of yours.

Tommy answered Well Seattle slim!

I am not as stupid as you think,

I know you're much the best snooker player then me but I would play you for ten thousand to your twenty thousand.

3315

The country boy wants s two for one.

I think that makes us even two for one

Seattle slim was surprised and looked at his two friends.

3320 Their eye went wide this is just what we been looking for.

And then they went to the side of the room for a talk.

They all agreed that the country boy just got lucky.

325   Slim you could have run off what all that was left anytime.
    Slim play the way you can and kick his ass.

    Ok Seattle slim said let's play him for all he has because we won't get another shot at him when I well clean the fucking table on him.
330   Slim asked how much cash we have got all three of us.
    They counted there cash out and agreed to give Tommy two for one odds.
    The three hustlers came up with thirty-five thousand cash and then told Tommy to put your put share if you got it.
    Seventeen thousand five hundred
335   Tommy emptied his pockets they must have counted his money
    Tommy had in his pocket because there was only had forty dollars left.
    After covering there bet.
    Tommy said Judy please give me that stick out of the old sack.

340   Tommy then said yes but the cash has to be put up on the bar let the bartender watch it.
    They agreed.
    The prize money was fifty-two thousand dollars total ($52.000.00 cash) setting on the bar.
    Judy almost fainted.
345   Then out of the old sack tommy on rapped the Diamond Brady queue the rear handle where the purple sapphire sparkled as the bar lights hit the sapphires
    Now Mr. slim had a close look at that stick.
    It somehow chook slim up just the site of it.
    Slim know that queue.
50   The gamble happens so fast only two games

    Never really had time to think things over it were all imputes.

    The cowboy was the underdog Seattle slim licked his lips. They were dry from (nerves)
55

    Tommy started screwed the diamond Brady together and all the champions that owed and used it seemed to come with it their spirits ran through Tommy could feel them.

    They lived through the sparkling purple sapphires the more they sparkled the better
60   tommy could shoot.

Tommy could feel them and all their talent came with that feeling there was a magical connection there?

(THE BIG GAME (ALL OR NOTHING)

3365

The flip of the coin
Tommy called tails the coin rolled and up came tails.
It was Tommy's break this was important to win the flip.

3370 Tommy could control slim somewhat shooting first.
Tommy looked at Seattle slim he could see a very serious shark looking right at Tommy it bothered Tommy slims burning eyes.

But Tommy past it off with an innocent carefree country boy grins.
3375 That bothered slim?
That intern bothered slim more even upset slim.
Slim know this was no street hustler it was a professional hit.
Directly directed at Seattle slim

3380 Tommy took sharp aim and shoot with smooth perfect wait ticked off a red just loosen up one red then rolled perfectly to the top of the table rested behind the brown ball.

Seattle slim was hocked on all balls never had a shot.
Slim tied to hit a red but miss's Tommy scored four.
3385 Then Tommy had an open shot at a red to the corner and made it set himself up for the black,
As tommy shot the black
Tommy put a smoking amount of side spin on the queue ball breaking out three more reds.
3390 Tommy professionally made five blacks.
Giving Tommy a big lead
Then taking no chances playing a safety leaving slim hocked at the top of the table.

Slim was starting to lose his composer saying fuck you are playing like an old woman.
3395 Then fats missed again Tommy was in control.
Until big Louis and Brother Leonard walked in and big Louis started looking around

seen that pile of cash on the bar and tommy and slim in a serious game!
  Big Louis started yelling that cash is our money and was going to grab it off the bar,
and then the bartender poked his pistol and Louis he stepped back.

400
    They both were bothering Tommy so much it through Tommy's game off,
  Tommy's control was gone.
  Then slim took over and ran most of the table before missing and easy shot
   Leaving Tommy, a very hard shot
405 Tommy had to backwards bank the ball across to the other side or play a safety.
  Tommy looked and in his mind said fucks it I am going for it.

  Then lined up called the shot.
  Looked up and slim he was ready to clean the table if Tommy missed.
410 Tommy shoot the red spun and bounced it was a thin slice

  Slim was about to start as the red still spinning and fell in the side pocket.
   Then Tommy ran the colored balls and the game was over.
  Tommy had defeated Seattle slim for real.

415

The glory of the win was overwhelming to Tommy.

  Then big Louis and Leonard made their move Leonard grabbed the cash as Judy tried to
  stop him.
420 Big Louis slapped Judy
   She fell as her wig fell off Judy was bald.
  That was another devastating flash she looked like Clancy the clown.

  Tommy was almost going to take her home to the ranch.
25 Then the bartenders almost shoot big Louis,

  Tommy ran over and yelled don't shoot them there my Brother and cousin.
  I don't need to go to anymore family funerals.
  Out the door they went with the cash.
30 Tommy helped Judy up and said thanks for trying she was putting on her wig.
  And trying to tell Tommy she couldn't stop him.
  Then we settled down and it was all over.
  Judy's wig was on crocked
  Tommy's heart was breaking and it wasn't the money.
35 The bartender set up two schooners and said there on the house.

Then the three sharks approached Tommy as he set at the bar.
Seattle slim said that was good shooting and I never seen your fucking hustle until you fucking had us.

3440 Where did you get that stick Seattle slim said I seen it before?
Tommy told slim that's my father' gave it to me when he challenges me and I run the table with a queue from off the wall.

Seattle Slim then asked who/s your daddy?
3445 Tommy said Bill Marks sir do you know him or heard of him.
Holly fuck, slim said your Billy Marks's kid
Tommy answered yes sir:

Slim said I know that fucking stick! Your dad won that stick from one of the best
3450 hustlers in the biz up in Vancouver young Billy Marks broke him and took that queue too.

Plus, Billy turned out to be the King Diamond Brady in 1933.

3455 The three pro hustlers smiled and said we live for the money and the hustle but we complement you on your set up style. Fats said half the hustle is the set up.
Your one of the best we ever seen just like your father
You have hustled before you're a pro.
You must have a handle every one that shoots has one.
3460
What's your street name country boy you play under?

Well Tommy said I really don't have one, but they call me the Cowboy Con man.

3465
Slim SAID WELL BOYS WE JUST GOT HUSTLED
BY THE COWBOY CON MAN!
No offence but we hope we never see you again in this life time!

3470 Slim and his two friends all wished Tommy well but said I never want to meet you on that pool table ever!
The cowboy and Judy were setting at the bar watching Slim and his partners left couldn't get out of there fast enough.

475   Judy and Tommy set at the bar cooling out.
      The cash was gone.
      The bartender said he never seen anything like this before.
      And set up two more shooters on the bar, and said it's on the house again.

480   Tommy and Judy thanked the bartender.

      Then the bartender asked can I get you picture cowboy. You're the best hustler I ever seen.
      I am putting you on the wall as one of the best hustlers (the Cow boy con man)
485

I was feeling sorry for you at the start Judy said.
The real hustlers you cleaned them out and now you just got robbed and you're broke.

      Tommy said give us another beer I still got twenty bucks.
490   The bartender said oh it's on the house again thanks sir.
      Tommy and Judy thanked the bartender for the cold beer.

      Then Tommy told Judy well sweetie it looks like it's over for now.
      I have to go back to the race track and face the consequences.
495   And go back the same way I came run back up the same tracks I ran down.

      Tommy will have to sleep on the two straw bales with those stinky old horse blankets.
      They better give me my earnings back but they're going to be mad as hell.

00   Tommy then told Judy that eight thousand dollars I used to start up with was Brother Leonard and big Louise.
      Judy said cowboy you don't need to go back
      I still got that fifteen hundred you gave me let's start over we can travel around and make a lot of money.
05   "Tommy please doesn't go."
      Well Judy it's not that simple.
      Tommy told Judy
      I must go face the music.
      But can you give me a number to call you.
10   Yes, Judy said and quickly wrote a number and she said its mom's phone number please call Tommy.
      Then Tommy stud up to leave the bartender said I am putting the cowboy con man's

picture behind the bar.
Please stop by again.

3515 Tommy said yes, I will and thanks.
Tommy was about to leave then Judy said hay Cowboy lets go have a nice beer and some bacon and eggs.
Judy gave Tommy a sad look.

3520 Tommy said you're paying

Judy put her arm around Tommy and said let's go to the restaurant Denny's.

Judy smiling then said The Cowboy con man is breaking but somehow it didn't bother
3525 the cowboy one bit.
The only thing that was bothering Tommy was Judy's wig it was on crooked.
Tommy said please go fix your hair.
Then asked her how come you lost your hair?
Then Judy said it just happens once every couple year… it will come back soon.

3530
Tommy said hope so.
They finished eating then Judy looked sad, she said you better call me.
Yes, Tommy said so as I clear the problems up.
We will see each other don't worry, and then Judy felt better.

3535
Judy said I will always remember the Cowboy with the purple sapphire queue called the Diamond Brady with all the champion spirits from past owners.

Judy said that fancy stick and the country boy con man has a way to work into the heart
3540 of a girl. And Judy said I wish that I could get some more of that magic stick of yours, but I guess time has run out for us.
Tommy then told Judy I'll come back and visit you shortly I promise. And thanks for the bacon and eggs. Good luck. Judy had to have one more hug. She held on for a long time Tommy letting her. (Tommy kissed her then pulled away.

3545
Judy then said I won't forget about you cowboy.
Looking back at the setup

Tommy, you coned everyone even me all the time you were evaluating the compaction
3550 even losing at the state line.
And that pearl handled purple sapphire class sticks with all those champion spirits in it

that was magical if it's true that made the events like the story of David and goliath.

Cowboy I'll never forget you!

555

Then Tommy left.
And ran back up the same old railway track and pulled the barn slates open and lay
down on the dirty old horse blankets and had a peaceful overdo sleep.

560   Before big Louie and Brother Leonard come.
This wasn't going to be nice.
The morning came quickly.

Brother Leonard and Louis were walking towards the stall ware I was sleeping.
565

Both were looking mad as hell, and called Tommy you little prick.
Then told Tommy come on let's go to the book keeper's the racing office.
We can't trust you enough to give you the money to deposit it.

570   We are claiming three race horses' tonight and maybe five tomorrow night average price
six thousand each tonight.
And five tomorrow average three thousand each.

Tommy said that's my money you're spending I'll look after you when we get back to
575   the ranch, Leonard said what would the old man think if I told him you stole big Louis
and my money.
Tommy, you would be kicked off the ranch.
You know Dad would never put up with a thief.

80   Tommy said ok but gave me some of that cash I played for it and won.
Leonard give Tommy forty dollars and told Tommy to be here and we need two people
to help cool the horses off after the race you can help cool the horse's out tommy.

Leonard and Louie pushes over fifty thousand dollars' worth of race horses
85   And never gave tommy only forty dollars.
When we got back to the ranch and unloading the horse.
Tommy asked witch horses are mine,
Leonard said here's your horse.

90   Then handed the lead rope to Tommy,

Tommy seeing this old the cheapest horse we claimed fifteen hundred dollars is all he cost.

Tommy was mad;

Leonard said he might be worth four thousand with some rest.

3595

Plus, you better shut up about the cost of the horse's and where the money came from remember Tommy you are a thief and Dad better not here of that so shut up.

3600

Dad and uncle Jack were real proud of Leonard's (smarts) going down to the United States and beating them out of fifty Grande, then investing it into fifty thousand worth of race horses.

Leonard was getting lots of respect from everyone.

3605

Until one Day Dad started thinking I raised Leonard to be responsible.

It just doesn't sound right dad was thinking Leonard would have never made a bet like that;

3610 He would never take that chance.   (Something is wrong)

Dad called big Louis to come over Dad wanted to ask him something.

Big Louis respected bill marks and would never lie to him.

3615

Luis walked into the kitchen and bill poured a coffee and then asked Louie just what happened down there.

How did Leonard get fifty thousand?

3620

Big Louie said I can't remember dad looked at Louis and then Louie said hers how it happened.

We gave Tommy eight thousand five hundred to deposit into the horseman's account but Tommy crawled out of the race track stall onto the railway tracks and ran away.

3625

Then we stood waiting for him outside the stall Tommy said he needed the piss.

We looked in and there were two boards polled apart and Tommy was gone.

Bill asked with that money.

Yes, Louis said. Leonard said that son of a bitch went pool hustling.

630 And Leonard was Wright. We rented an old Volkswagen and drove bar to bar looking for him and tommy was sometimes ten minutes ahead of us.

Dad ask what did the people in the bars say about him Louis said oh they all said he was one of the best pool hustlers they ever seen.
635 We never clout of with him for five days until we got a tip there was a big money game going on at a palace bar called Girds. We walked in and their Tommy was had every cent bet total $52.000. 00 dollars sitting on the bar
Tommy had that fancy stick of your Bill.

640 Then that was for all that cash Tommy had every cent of the money tommy made with our money plus every cent of our cash was on the bar too. Total cash $52.000.00

Dad set back in his chair and asked was Tommy using that Diamond Brady stick.
 Louis said yes sir. Louis said did tommy still that too.
645

Dad then asked did Tommy win easy.
No sir we were raising hell trying to get our money out of that bet.
Tommy made with our money we interrupted the game.

650 Tommy almost lost but finish the guy called Seattle slim off.

Then Leonard and I grabbed all the cash and made a fast exit the bartender was going to shoot us but tommy stopped him.

655 When we got back to the motel we counted it and there was $52.000.00 USA cash there we never know there was that much cash there to start with.

Dad then asked Leonard you never gave Tommy his winnings.
No Louis said, Leonard keep saying Tommy' stole our money and was using it to
660 gamble with.

Tommy stole your money.
OK Louis" Bill said thanks for telling me the truth about what happen I knew Leonard never made a big gamble he is to responsible he would never take that chance.
665 But Tommy would I knew it Bill said.

Bill Marks after hearing that story about Tommy using the Diamond Brady and naturally hustling those sharks at some shark tank palace in Spokane.

3670 Bill got a cold beer out of the fridge walked into the living room and set down in his chair.
There came a lump in Bills throat and tears in his eyes,
Billy was thinking of when he used that Diamond Brady to Win the King Diamond Brady championship in 1933 in Baltimore and the glory full moment that was.

3675
Billy whispered I know it would come out sometime but what a strange way it came?

Bill was proud of young Tommy.

3680 Bill waited until the next day to talk to Leonard this must be straightened out and Bill thought it over very carefully.
Tommy did steal their money? Or borrowed it?

After lunch Bill said to Leonard and Tommy both of you come into the study with a
3685 serious tone.
Dad set in his chair looked at both of us in discuss.
Dad said I know the truth about where the cash came from it wasn't made by you cashing a big gamble Leonard.
And Tommy how you could steal their money like that
3690 Tommy answered I didn't steal it I just used it. Old bill said, Well Tommy you should never use anybody's money to hustle with but your own.

You went into that horse stall told your brother and cousin you need to pee,

3695 Then you crawled out the back and ran downtown Spokane with their cash.

Why did you do that… old Bills eyes were burning Tommy.
Tommy said I never had anything to eating no money and was sleeping in that stall for over two weeks.
3700 I looked like a bum and Leonard wouldn't give me any money even to clean up with they had nice suits on I was a stable boy.

Plus, they wouldn't even take me to eat with them,

3705 Dad asks Leonard why you didn't look after your little brother, Leonard was on the spot right now.
Then dad said to Leonard you invented a big story about you cashing a big gamble just

to steal Tommy's winnings and make yourself look good and lied.

710 The both of you learned you're to always look after each other.
 Well that's not working stop both of you.
 Leonard no more lies.
 Tommy, you don't ever take money that's not yours, never go hustling with some one else's money.
715

 Ok Leonard you're going to make things more even you're going to give Tommy ten thousand cash and do it today.
 And you big Louis stop trying to bully Tommy,
I can see that won't last much longer anyway.
720

Leonard was mad and said I am not giving Tommy one cent.
Dad was mad, then said get all those horse papers and gives all those horses to Tommy.
then Leonard, ok I'll give him the ten thousand then we are all clear.

725 Then said I'll get the ten thousand today.
 Then Dad said this is settled both of you start cooperating with each other.

And I don't want to hear about this again or anything like this!
The next day Dad called Tommy to come to the house and they both had a cup of black
730 coffee.
Dad asked who did you skinned out of the fifty Grande sons.
Tommy told dad it was a fat guy called Seattle slim.
 He knows your dad.
 He seen the Diamond Brady and asked where I got it?
35

 Yes, dad said
Tommy if you can hustle the likes of Mr. Seattle slim you're a lot more than a street hustler
. Tommy asked how good is Seattle slim.
40 Dad told Tommy the only season slim was in a small place like Spokane is everyone knows him it's hard for slim to hustle for any big bucks when he is known slim he has won several big champion ships. He is one of the best on the west coast

 Then he ran into a hot young hustler called young Tommy Marks.
45 OK Bill said save that ten thousand Leonard gave you.

Old Bill Marks 46 years' he knows the ropes

3750

And I'll loan you another ten thousand and you got another twenty thousand don't you Tommy.

Tommy replied yes Dad I'll do my best.

That's around forty thousand for your trip if you lose that your retired Tommy

3755

Old Bill smiled and told Tommy I am going to give you a map of places to go.

Tommy you're going to come home broke and if that happens you 're finished with shooting snooker.

I want you to come back with at least one hundred thousand in your pocket.

3760 Tommy you're going to play the finest hustlers in the world remember.

Keep that innocent country boy way mannerisms and talk slow.

"And don't ever start thinking you're the best".

That's when you will go down,

3765 Remember Tommy it's all inside you and don't let anyone of those hustlers over dominate you that make them think they got you Tommy manipulation and outsmart them?

Play it just the way you are.

770 Wait until the work is finished on the ranch then you will go now start thinking snooker get the spin and your English to go inches way from where you want that queue ball to be" get sharp "Dad said over and over.

The hustlers you're going to be playing will take every bit of your cash you have and everything you will ever have if they can.
775 "So be ready Tommy."

Go finish the ranch work.
They are looking for a country hick to take all your cash.
They are brutal (Tommy you better be ready!)
780 But if you're as good as I think you are there going to regret the day they laid their eyes on you!
Then old Bill smiled wandering if Tommy would hold up to the east coast sharks?
Old bill figured Tommy has no nerves nothing bothers him, (Tommy should clean house)

785
Chapter 15-
The work around the ranch was almost finished.
Dad was putting together Tommy's map of places to hustle or get hustled.

All the winter feed was put into large stacks and the first snow had come.
790 It was time for Tommy to go.

There was a Christmas dance in Lomond. it was a community gets to gather mom and dad demanded we all attend.
And then Tommy would go on his most important trip of his life Tommy was sent after
95 the best hustlers in the world.

At the country dance cousin, big Louie was starting to get drunk. Louis and Leonard were drinking some clear moon shine they bought from some old drunk that lived over by the lake.
00 The two of them were starting to act up. It was funny at first but big Louie was getting drunk all six-foot-tall of him and the two hundred and fifty pounds too.

Big Louie was starting to bully some of the locals.

05 It was escalating into an old fashion donnybrook it seemed every time big Louie had a

few too many he would start throwing his weight around and everyone was scared of his size.

Then mom even got into it with Louie.

That was the end when Louie told mom to mind her own biz.

3810 Louie was big and a mild mannered until he drank with the moon shiners.

Tommy jumped up and asked Louis to come out side and we will settle this.

Big Louie said Tommy I have wanted to do this for a long time you little prick stealing
3815 my cash in Spokane.

Then up Louie jumped and out the dance hall we went.

Big Louie was big and strong.

Tommy peppered Louie in the head many times. Big Louis would make hard powerful
3820 swings that only struck air,

Big Louis could not catch Tommy.

Then Tommy threw out six punches hitting Louie every one hitting the face and temple.

3825 Tommy was not in one place he kept moving circling Louis making the big man move the way Louis didn't want to turn.

Louis was behind Tommy all the time.

It was a massacre, big Louie had to stop, both eyes were swelled shut.
3830 Big Louie was too slow.

The fight was over and we all jumped into the truck and road back to the ranch, mom and Dad in the front and us boys in the truck box.

In two days Dad went over to Louis farm to see if he was OK.

3835

Louis was embarrassed… no one seen him for three days, and that was strange.

This was not big Louis way. There was defiantly something wrong and dad new it.

3840 It turned out that big Louie had a loan on his farm for fifteen thousand dollars.

The bank in Vulcan was for closing on Louis farm.

Dad knew the greedy bank and their managers. They are ruthless.

845 Mom said Louis's farm is worth three times that isn't it.
Dad answered it worth ten times that fifteen thousand ((greedy bankers)

Dad answered, that greedy banker needs a little snake valley justice.
Mom smiled knowing when Bill said that something was up?
850

CHAPTER 16

Dad called Louis and told Louis to wait, dad had to think for a couple days.

855 Then dad would let Louis know what to do,

Dad told Louis you're not going to lose your ranch,
I will figure something out; those bankers are getting too greedy.

860 Old Bill Marks explained to mom what was happening to Louis, and she said that's terrible can't the bank give Louis a little more time?

Instead of foreclosing and taking Louis farm its worth away more than fifteen thousand.

865 Bill said yes it sure is but those banks want to make lots of profit on every deal they make.
Mom said Bill you can't let that happen.
Bill said honey I have a plane.
On the third day, old bill drove over to big Louis farm.
870
There Louis was sitting there upset losing his farm with no way out of it.
I can't pay that fifteen thousand Louis said.
Old Bill said call that banker and tell him you have the cash to pay the loan off in full!

875 Old Bill said Louis "tell that greedy banker you saved it and it is your life savings.
Luis said then what?

Old bill said tell the banker to come out tomorrow at twelve sharp.
You will be waiting for him with the cash.
880 Tell him you will go dig it up.
And to be here at twelve noon.

Bill said call right now, and tell that greedy bastard to bring a letter of payment in full document directly from the bank or you won't pay it.

3885

OK Louis called the greedy banker.
The banker answered.
Louis what can I do for you Louis? Louis told the banker exactly what Bill told him to say.

3890 Louis had his life savings and would dig it up and pay the banker if he would come out to retrieve to cash in turn bring a paid in full receipt from the bank.
The banker didn't believe Louis had that much saved up.
Louis said I will dig it up and count it out to you personally.

3895 Louis said I don't trust you Mr. Banker… make sure you bring that receipt. The banker said OK Louis, I'll be there with a full receipt paid in full with a bank stamp or his sig. But if there's no cash I will be bringing that for closer document and it reeds final notice.

3900 That means in thirty days' that farm is owned by the bank.
And you must move on!
Louis was being coached by dad. Dad whispered tell him you have all the cash please tell me the exact amount please Louis asked what the exact amount he owes is.
The banker said its fifteen thousand six hundred and thirty dollars. And I will be at your
3905 ranch at one pm tomorrow.

Then Louis hung the phone up and looked at old Bill now. What Louis said.

Old bill said Louis I'll bring the fifteen thousand six hundred and thirty dollars over
3910 around ten tomorrows you stay home and make sure you get that paid in full receipt with the banker's stamp and his signature on it from that bank manager. Before you give him the cash!
Louis said yes sir I'll make sure of that Bill.
If you don't receive the stamp and signature don't give that crock any money!
3915 Remember Louis you're dealing with a fucking swindler… be sharp! He will try and keep those documents!
Louis said I heard you no cash until the singed paper.

3920

THE EVIL BANKER

EARLY the next day-old Bill drove over to Louis farm it was around nine.

925 Gave Louis a bag of cash it was all twenties and one-dollar bills even change.

But there was fifteen thousand six hundred and thirty dollars there!

Old bill said it would take that greedy banker and hour just to count it.

930 Louis said thanks.
Then old Bill reminded Louis again dont give him anything without that stamp and his signature!
Yes, Louis said I got that Bill.
Then old Bill drove out of Louis farm and back to his ranch.
935 He rounded up Leonard and Tommy and gave them their orders. Viola came with city clothes for both and told the boys to put on the city suits and shoes.

No Tommy said my suites don't fit… Leonard said the same.
Mom told the boy just make do with them, role the pants up.
940 .

Old Bill said ware the city suits boys along with the hats… they are called fedoras then old Bill told the boy's what to do.

There was an old wooden bridge over a small creek, just before the main road on Louis
945 drive way.
Tommy and Brother Leonard set under the bridge waiting for the banker to drive into Louis ranch,
The banker drove over the bridge real slow probably not trusting the bridge because it was so old.
50 Leonard and Tommy ran around and pulled off one of the bridge planks and turned it over so the spikes were turned up.
The spikes would wreck all the bankers' tires if he hit them and it would be hard to miss them.
The banker was counting the cash and big Louie was watching every move.
55

It came to fifteen thousand and fifty dollars the banker said that's the right amount.
Louis said, give me back the cash Louis grabbed the cash from the banker.

The banker said in a snoot fully jester… It's against the law to keep the queens cash
3960   under a stone or where ever you keep this. Louis, I am going to tell the police about this.
Trying to scare big Louis

Big Louis was mad telling the banker wares the receipt?
The little greedy banker could see Louis meant it.
3965

He stopped and angrily singed and stamped a receipt.

Then Louis stuck out his hand to shake hands with the banker, but the banker declined
and told big Louis his credit was bad and to never come into the bank again.
3970

The banker started driving back to Vulcan.
In the meantime, the banker was smiling he added one thousand more than Louis really
owed, then the banker pocketed the thousand.
Tommy and Leonard were waiting under the old bridge;
3975   The banker's car was traveling fast he wanted away from Louis ranch.

His car hit the spikes hard then spun sideways skidding on all four-tires flattened
running only on the rims.
The banker opened the car door and was looking at all the damage to the back of his
3980   own car, all four tires were blown.
Leonard carefully climbed over the bridge rail on the opposite side. the brief case was
sitting on the front seat!
Leonard grabbed it and throws it down to Tommy then Leonard started to climb back
over the bridge railing.
3985   Tommy was into the willow trees and halfway out of site.
Leonard wasn't far behind; the banker saw Leonard from though the trees.
They kept running. they stopped a mile away in the trees. Leonard looked
In the leather bag said let's count that cash.
Tommy said OK.
3990   Leonard had two piles of cash, it sure was fun to count it.
We finished counting and there was twenty-five thousand there ten thousand more that
Big Louis gave the banker.

Leonard said we better go show Dad.
3995   Leonard and Tommy started running back home to the ranch, it was around four miles.
Dad was waiting.
Leonard told Dad there's more money in the banker's bag then big Louis gave him.

Dad smiled and took the brief case; holy smokes Dad said there's twenty-five thousand in here.

Dad then said the greedy banker must have been collecting from more ranchers!

OK boy's Dad said start a fire in the garbage barrel
Dad took all the cash out of the bag and put it in his coat pocket.
Then burned the banker's papers and his brief case.

Dad told Tommy and Leonard to never say anything about this too anybody.
In a few days' there were two police driving into our ranch! They knocked on the house door, it was lunch time.
Mom answered the door and invited the two police men inside.
Dad said, hello officers, what can I do for you?
The two police men asked, did you see any city people around here in the last few days?
Mom said yes there was a pot and pan salesman here two days ago.

The police officer asked, was he was wearing a black suite?
Yes, mom said with one of those city hats called fedoras or something like that.

Then the police asked, what kind of car was he driving, mom said I never noticed.
Then dad asked, what this is all about?
The police said, oh there's been another city robbery.
We will report what you seen miss's Marks, bye, have a good day.

When they were gone big Louis came in and we shared the cop's investigation,
Dad told Louis they seen a guy running that resembled you Louis. Louis looked serious, but we all started laughing.
It was over, Louis got his farm back and we made ten thousand just like finding it on the street.
All worked for around two weeks' no one saying anything about Louis and the greedy banker.
Then one-day Dad came out and gave us the news.
Well boy's i just heard the news about the greedy banker.
Leonard and Tommy's ears came up.
Bill said, how did you two run with the cash and never left any tracks?
Leonard started thinking... well we jumped off the bridge onto the gravel, then ran through the willows, and the willows are under water right now.
We ran down the creek in the water.

Dad said good thinking boy's if those police could have followed your track, we would be in trouble… good thinking!

4040 The bank and the police didn't believe the bankers story about two city people coming around with suits on someone would have seen them and their car.

The police checked all the gas stations out that day and nobody seen any city people.

The bank found out the greedy employee had an old habit of stealing a few bucks out of
4045 the bank.

Then big Louis had the stamped and signed receipt. Proof that Louis paid the bank note off.

They fired the greedy thief.

4050 Old Bill smiled and said boy's I think he got just what he deserved, trying to take big Louis farm for around 20% of what it was worth.

We all laugh and it felt great.

It was over.
4055 The next day-old Bill told Tommy to start shooting snooker and Old Bill would shoot with him to sharpen Tommy up.

Then mom said Bill…

Tommy can't go any ware dressed like a cowpoke.

4060 Mom said she would go to Lethbridge and buy Tommy some new cloths.

When is Tommy leaving Bill?

Oh, Bill said… in two weeks. I have a few more words of advice. This is the most important trip of Tommy's life.

He is going to the hottest billiard shooters in the world!
4065 Tommy must be ready.

Tommy needs some well-dressed city type white shirts.

Then dad changed his mind. Dad said maybe Tommy should keep the cowboy style new cowboy hat Fancy dancing boots and a new suite case!

4070

CHAPTER-17-
The big Hustle New York to Delaware then Baltimore
075   Dads told Tommy go make your mark son or be a cowboy!
But being a Cowboy is still a good life.

A few days later Dads made a list of places for Tommy to go and was explaining every place, what all the billiard halls looked like, and when he was there in 1933 to 1936.
080   It was many years later… 1972 now.

The first place on the list was east Cicero Chicago.

The places in this neck of the woods Dad said is mostly Italian.
085   Your Irish so be careful. They don't like Irish and Tommy you even look Irish!

If they see you're a hustler in Cicero they'll let you think you're putting one over on them.
But in the last minute they will rob you and kick the living shit out of you!
090   There are no Irish friends there. Maybe you better not waste any time there!... Be careful!

And Tommy never used the house chalk. Their trick is to put acid in the chalk and it will eat the leather queue up slowly enough that it will throw you off and make you
095   miss.
Watch out for every dirty trick in the book there.
Maybe get out of it quickly.

Next stop… If you survive Chicago there is a part of New York called Manhattan.
00

If you make it that far before you're broke, remember to keep enough cash for bus fare home.
I am not sending you any travailing money, always keep a little start over cash hidden.

05   Tommy, when you get to Manhattan, tell them your mother is Irish. That will get you in some doors… tell them she is a Donnelly. Then later tell them your grandfather changed it to Donily. They might remember your Grande father Ore Donily.
You might run into your cousins there.

4110 Tommy… people in New York always think they're the best at everything and most of the time it's true! Be ready for that and take advantage of it!

Tommy be extra careful there because that old part of Manhattan is still called Hell's Kitchen… it's all Irish mafia… very powerful people.

4115 Tommy try and be real friends with your family there. Don't lie to them or try and set them up. Play that hustler style you just don't know? Let them decide you're not that good. Then win.

Tommy your cousins name is Donnelly spelled different then your moms (Donily). Your 4120 grandfather wanted away from that reputation of mafia.

But he operated like them only in Chicago.
They run Manhattan and Manhattan runs New York Tommy. It's the Irish mafia's home.

4125 They are your blood relations, don't try and take their money.

Try and be friends. Tell them your mother's maiden name is Donily.

There's an old classic snooker hall there called Polo Billiards and Bowling Alley.
4130
That's where most of the money snooker players hang out. Its located in old Manhattan the (hell's kitchen area).
Believe me Tommy, you be ready for anything there!

4135 "Yes sir "! Tommy answered with eyes wide open and listening

Next go to Wilmington Delaware, go to a part called (Brown Town). It alive there!
Bookies and gambling houses everywhere. You might get lucky there.
Remember those bookie houses will take bets from anywhere on almost anything!
4140
The last on the list is the true test!

There's a night club called the California Inn.
All the named shooters are there or coming through.
4145
Old Bill said, bet those big shot bastards!

Tommy, if you make it through all this….

150   You will be very famous and have their cash in your pocket!

They will over dominate you, make you feel one inch tall.
Tommy, old Bill said, you be strong… I beat them in 1933! I won and lost.

155   But I won more than I lost. Tommy l always won at the right time somehow.
Tommy… don't worry… you can always come home; the cowboy life is good.

I hope everything I taught you works for you. You certainly have the confidence
You're excellent at it as far as I see.
160   Before Avery match, get lots of sleep, rest your eyes… there you're most important
weapons.

Get lots of sleep.
Dad said Tommy my boy, you're stepping into the lion's den!
165

Now Tommy when you win some cash, please send it back to me at the ranch.

I will buy you more cows, then you will have something when you get older.
Keep your eye open for everything; you're strong enough to beat big Louie and big john
70   coal you're ready for anyone.

The next morning, mom was getting ready for shopping in Great Falls, Montana.
Mom and Dad jumped into the car and off we went to the bus depot in Great Falls
Montana.
75   It was around two hundred fifty miles from the ranch.
They both had so much advice on the way there, it almost drove Tommy crazy.
Dad would say watch for this and that.
Then mom said would say Tommy you don't know about those girl's. Mom said they
will lie to you, rob you.
80   Watch out for them Tommy.
Was Tommy ever happy to see the bus depot! It was on a large hill in Great Falls
Montana.
We waited for two hours. An old yellow bus drove in with Chicago in the window.
That's it! said Dad, we all ran to the bus as if it would fly away!
85   We were all excited, Dad said, I hope this don't turn out disastrous!
Mom was still saying watch those girls Tommy.

The old bus started up… mom had tears, dad I could tell he was really concerned.

The old bus… a bunch of smoke poured out, gears grinded and away it went.

4190 The dust was coming inside the bus. It was terrible. Soon, it hit a narrow road that was called black top.
It took three days to get to Chicago.
Tommy was so tired and dirty, he needed a shower and some sleep.

4195
Chapter 18-
CHICAGO EAST CICERO

In two days Tommy would be in Chicago and he would go strait the east Cicero.
The place Dad said be careful.
The old bus was very uncomfortable. Tommy only slept a few hours in two days.

4200 The site of the big city of Chicago… man it was a big Plus! the skyscrapers were everywhere!

He couldn't stop thinking about those hustling girl's mom told Tommy about.
The bus was finally arriving at central station… Chicago central. Tommy had never

4205 seen a big city! he was amazed! Tommy was lost all the time… when he asked a passerby for directions, they looked at Tommy strange and kept walking.
It was a new experience. People did not talk and they looked upset when you spoke to them.

4210 Tommy finally took a cab to east Cicero, and check into the Sheraton hotel.
Tommy ate supper then went straight to bed.

The next day in Chicago, Tommy slept until twelve noon.
He went, had coffee, and went out onto the street of east Cicero. He started checking

4215 out small bars and some big poker rooms.
They all had something in common… they all had a big poker room and pictures of big ell Capone hanging on their walls!
This was big AL's home territory, I mean ell Capone. Joe Kennedy gave the five Capone brothers thirty minutes to get out of New York, or they would be shot down like

4220 dogs!
So… the Capone's left New York to Chicago.

There wasn't much for snooker tables, but one thing interested Tommy in every bar…
the poker players all had around five thousand to ten thousand dollars sitting in front of
225 them!

Tommy noticed they must be playing table stakes only.
he was looking for the easiest table of poker face players.
Tommy was going to try his sleight of hand. He went into a convenience store and
230 purchased a deck of cards.
Tommy went back to the Sheridan hotel and started practicing with the deck.
He wasn't confident with some of his moves, this would take more time.
Tommy watched several games and was searching for the ones with the most cash on
the table.
235 But here's what tommy had to work with… he could pull any card from the first five
cards on the top of the deck plus the bottom. Everyone watches the bottom of the deck
so it was safer to take from the top only.

This gave him an eight-card advantage.
240

Tommy loved small cards. Tommy had it figured out. There were so many ways to build
a wining hand working with the small card straits, Low ball hands and even a better
chance at a strait flush or three or four of a kind!

245 Tommy could almost get a card from inside the deck, but not quite yet.

He also noticed that all the poker players had their entire stack of cash on the table.
He knows they were playing table stakes only.

50 Meaning nobody could dig into his pocket.

Maybe cheat in some way or another.
Tommy noticed that the hard-faced poker players that smoked were digging for their
lighters and cigarettes all the time.
55 Tommy pushes a pack of cigarettes called Lucy's. Red and white little box with two
penny matches.

Tommy practiced for two hours in a dark café and waited for the late night.
Things always loosened up then… popped in a cigarette, and were trying to get used to
60 it so it would look natural for Tommy… He had to look like a smoker.

The cards wore working much better. Tommy came to play snooker not poker.

THE GAME

4265   Tommy chickened out and said I'll shoot some snooker see if there's anyone with some cash.

All the snooker joints were empty.

But there were a few small timers around. Tommy went joint to joint and made around three hundred… There was nothing in Cicero for snooker.

4270

AN old man wandered into the poker den… Tommy was watching.

The old grumpy poker player said ether sit and play or get to fuck out of here kid.

So, Tommy sat at the far corner.

They dealt Tommy in and said, do you know the rules kid?

4275

Tommy said, why no sir, I only played poker on the farm.

Well its table stakes… put you betting cash on the table.

Tommy said OK and only put up five hundred to their stacks of at least ten thousand!

4280   All the rest had at least ten thousand or more.

The first-hand… Tommy got excited and said I'll take two cards sir.

Way before it was Tommy's turn.

All the poker face players got mad and said don't you ever do that again, wait until it's your turn… where have you been? Everyone knows that.

4285

There were old gamblers that said why did you let the kid in? he doesn't even know how to play.

Tommy tried to win the first hand but only had five hundred to bet tommy was over bet quickly, so there was a side pot.

4290   Tommy won fifteen hundred in the side pot.

Now tommy had two thousand.

It was Tommy's deal now. Tommy called a game called 52. It was five cards down, one card at a time, bet each card up to five cards and then two one card draws.

It was the best out of seven cards. This gave Tommy lots of time to see what was in his

4295   hand and to smoothly get what he needed to win.

Tommy quickly was out of cash. His two thousand was in another side pot. Tommy won that. Tommy's cash on the table grew to six thousand quickly.

The owner of the last place Tommy was shooting snooker just walked into the bar and
300 was speaking to the big Italian manager and his two Italian bouncers.
They stormed into the poker room and came straight to Tommy. The big fat manager
said to Tommy...
Mr., we just got the word on you. There's a good man out in Seattle we know, and he
said you're a big-time hustler! you're a little bastard!
305

Both big Italian bouncers grabbed Tommy.
Tommy had just enough time to grab the cash off the poker table. Just then, one fat
Italian had Tommy by the neck, the other had Tommy's belt. To throw Tommy out in
the air, on to the cement sidewalk outside the bar.
310

They both told Tommy if they see him around in two hours, he would get the baseball
bat treatment.
We just got the word from an honest man slim.
Tommy said I don't know any slim. Oh yes you do! says the manager. You just skinned
15   him out of fifty thousand not more than a couple months ago!

Tommy got up but the cement skinned both elbows on the landing and one knee on
the cement sidewalk. He walked away limping back to the Sheraton hotel.

20   Back at the bar, the manager went into the poker room and all the poker players were
mad as hell! they said what in hell did you do that for! We seen the kid count his cash
and he had over ten thousand in his pocket!!!
We were just about to take the kids money. He doesn't even know how to play the
game! It would have been easy! Why did you throw him out like that?
25

Then the fat Italian manager said, You guys were about to get feasted out of every cent
plus your car's and everything!
He is a professional hustler his name is The Cowboy Con Man. An old friend called...
Seattle slim identified him.
30   The poker players looked at each other and said he convinced me.
Then the manager said that's his game!

Tommy was in the Sheridan hotel. He called the desk and asked, is there a bus or train to New York tonight? The desk clerk said, I will call... wait and I will call you with the info.

4335

In five minutes, the desk called and told Tommy... yes there's a red eye leaving in one hour. If you want to catch that train you will have to hurry!

4340 OK tommy said. I'll come right now. Can you arrange a ticket? The clerk said that the train is only walk on and its never full. I'll send for a taxi. Thanks Tommy said. I am on my way to the lobby.
Tommy wanted out of Chicago. It was the most unfriendly place he ever seen.
Tommy was off to New York!

4345

BY the time it took tommy to pack up and walk to the lobby the cab was waiting, he tipped the clerk, and into the cab tommy went.
Looking around for any Italians with baseball bats,
The cab pulled into the classiest terminal Tommy ever seen! White pillars, marble

4350 floors... man, Tommy was amazed and couldn't stop looking around. He purchased a one-way ticket to central station, New York

As the red eye was pulling out from Chicago terminal Tommy whispered, fuck Chicago and gave a finger through the window thinking about those baseball bats and big fat

4355 Italians.

4360

CHAPTER-19-

New York City central station

The New York family

Tommy finally went to sleep setting up on the train. There was a man that had a coffee

cart. and in doing so, woke up every passenger asking if they would have wanted a wake-up coffee.

Tommy said yes black please. Then asks the man how much longer to New York? Well, in twenty minutes we will be entering the out skirts of New York.

Tommy was excited first time in the big apple.

The train was entering New York City, Tommy was ready to see central station.

But the city was so big it took another hour through the city, to get to central station

the announcer said last stop central station... keep to the right of walk way.

Tommy followed the crowd and there it was. It had a cathedral ceiling with angel's, devils with horns, and several other thinks on the ceiling.

Then Tommy seen the action on the main floor.
Tommy stood at the top on the stairs watching the hustlers and pick pockets and the robbers.
On the way down the Grand elegant stairs, he was watching the crowd and to the side of the stairs there was a small old black man with a shoe shine bench waiting for

costumers to sit while he shines their shoes.

Tommy sat down and the old man said Hello cowboy, he asked, where you from son?

Tommy said, I got a cabin in the Rocky Mountains. Then he said, that's all the way out

west? Yes, sir Tommy answered.
Shoe shine Tommy eyed the crowd trying to figure out exactly what Tommy had to deal with.

4400 Tommy seen people with yellow and green hair, people with no shoes, some just street bums but Tommy seen two pick pockets partnering up one drew the marks attention the other picked him clean.

Tommy saw them clean two people in the last five minutes.
Then tommy seen to the far outer circle there were several street gangs watching like
4405 vultures.

The old black shoe shine man said that will be two dollars' cowboy; Tommy slipped him five and told him to keep the change.
Then the old man had some advice, Son go to that young black man standing halfway
4410 up the stairs to the street.
Give him twenty and you will get out of here safely... he is the boss here.
Tommy said thanks Mr. and walk strait to the young black boss and when tommy got close, their eyes met.
 Tommy passed a twenty on to his closed hand. He opened his hand and smiled.
4415
 The young black man winked and yelled and pointed to Tommy.
Out of central station he went "man what a trap.
Tommy hailed a cab. The cab stopped. Tommy asked how much to Polo Billiards over to old hell's kitchen?
4420 The response was his eye widened and drove off.
The second car pulled up, Tommy asks the same.
 The cab driver said no son. I don't go to that area unless I half to... and I don't have to!!! and drove off.

4425 Since Tommy never know where to go.
 There was an old dinner across from central park.
Tommy went in and ordered a coffee.
Tommy asked the waitress in the dinner, miss how can I get to Polo Billiards in old hell's kitchen in Manhattan?
4430 The waitress looked at Tommy and said you're not from around, here are you?
Tommy said no first are better be Irish! tommy said yes.
 OK she said then walked away like a New York cockroach.

Then an old man sitting beside me explained.
4435 When someone asks you are you Irish that means your mafia.

No, I am not but I might know some of them.
The old man asked, can you tell me your friend's last name?
Yes, Tommy said Donnelly sir.

140

The old man spits his coffee all over the counter.
Then said, I'll take you to Polo Billiards son. Come on the old man said.
We went out into the back ally and there was an old car all rusted up... he said get in.

145 Tommy threw his bag in the back, then away we went. The old man never said anything
but when we got to a street corner in old Manhattan, he pointed down the street
there's polo billiards.
Tommy said thanks and threw him twenty. The old man then said, you will meet me
later and you're a spitting image of your cousin!

50

That's the only reason I drove you here!
And I see you have a pool Queue with you!

Son don't go into Polo Billiards thinking you can pull a country boy hustle son... your
55 walking into the lion's cage! these old hell's kitchen hustlers will take everything from
you, even your shoes!!!
You're wasting your time son. Then after that advice he drove off.

Tommy stood half a block from Dad's legendary polo billiards. It looks just like Dad had
60 told Tommy.

Then Tommy stood at the big front doors and a thrill went through Tommy's body as
he entered!
It was full almost every table was taken.

65

Right away, the waitress asks Tommy, what I can get for your sir?

Tommy orders an ice tea.
When the waitress returned, she said where you are from sir?
70 Tommy told her he was from Alberta Canada and yes, I am Irish but just in blood not
mafia. OH, the waitress said that's OK.

Tommy watched the winners at the first three tables play. They all looked very good.

4475   The waitress returned. Tommy could tell she was sent by the bar tender.

She asked what your Irish name sir.
Tommy told her my mother is a Donily (Donnelly) She never said anything. She went straight back to the bar tender and told him Tommy's mothers name.

4480

The bartender quickly made a call.
And told someone that there is a young man using their name

IT wasn't ten minutes... in walked a young man with a beautiful girl with him.

4485

He went straight to the bar tender and asks who is using our name.

The bar tender pointed straight at tommy.

4490   They both looked and started walking towards him.

The girl stopped and said, he looks like he could be your brother!
Both stopped and starred at Tommy. They asked, why are you using that name Donnelly? Tommy said my mother is a Donily, the girl then said he looks like your

4495   brother Tom.
Then he asks, what's your name? Tommy answered. Tommy Marks Doily sir, and what's your name? He replied almost the same as yours.

Then Tom asked where you are from? Tommy said Alberta Canada.

4500

Tom asks can we join you? Tommy said yes. We sat and talked for an hour or so and then tom went and made a call.

When tom came back to the table, he said you're coming home to talk to Dad and

4505   mom and have supper with us. OK, Tommy agreed.

Tom then asks, why did you come here for? the big apple?
Tommy answered I came here to play snooker.

Tommy asks Tom, do you know the players in here?

510

Yes, Tom said I know everyone.

Tommy asked, well tell me who's got money in their pocket (boldly)!!!
Tom answered. OK there's a good shooter Tom pointed to a slick looking guy shooting
515 and he was winning too.
Tom said try him with a grin?
Tommy when and put a dollar on his table challenging his table looked and said OK
country boy what's you wager?
Tommy racked the balls and the same old hustle came out of his mouth.
20 I only play for fifty a game. Tommy said I don't have that much sir, the hustler said OK
just how much you got? Tommy said twenty.

The hustler said one game then but don't challenge my table again.
The hustler broke. The hustler didn't play very well thinking Tommy was a punk country
25 bumpkin.
The first game went Tommy's way and it was easy game for Tommy.
The second game went even easier for him.
Then the third they played for one hundred, and that was like shooting fish in a barrel.
Tommy had taken one hundred and fifty dollars from the New York street hustler.
30
The street hustler said, OK one game and he pulled for all the cash he had in his pocket.
He came up with four hundred; he said have you got the guts to play for that?

Tommy easily matched the four hundred not saying a word.
35 Tommy broke the balls and ran half of the table and then taking no chances played a
safety.
The street hustler was mad and yelled, you play chicken snooker country boy!
Tommy said please sir, call me cowboy.
The street hustler missed.
40 Than it was easy for him to clean the rest of the table.

That street hustler's voice changed after he lost his four hundred and asked please that
was my rent money! Mr. please loan it back!

45 Tommy said you should not gamble if you can't afford it, plus you run your mouth like

you were the champ.

Then Tommy walked back to Tom and his beautiful girl friends table.

Well I just won at least a week's rent, somewhere in Manhattan.

Tom said with a smile, there's a lot better shooter around than him Tommy. Around

4550 here

You better be careful. Tommy smiled.

Tom said well let's go and talk to mom and Dad and figure out if we are related.

 Yes, Sir Tommy said.

4555 And Out the pool hall door we went. To Tommy's surprise Tom had a limo waiting.

 Tommy said well this is the way to move in New York city, its better then a New York

cab I never rode in one of these before all we have is pickup trucks back at the ranch.

They work for everything! funerals and weddings.

Tom just got in and never said anything.

4560 We drove straight through old Manhattan Irish neighborhood, then we entered a

guarded huge old mention.

Tommy's mouth dropped open.

 Wow this is where you live?

 Tom nodded his head.

4565 The guard opened the gate and smiled at Tom as we went by.

Tom was met by an old butler that said, is that your Canadian cousin Tom?

Tom said, maybe... we half to talk to him. Mom and Tom senior will know.

Well welcome Tommy! the butler greeted Tommy graciously. Tommy said thank you.

4570 Inside a beautiful marble entrance, the butler said please follow me.

We walked into a room called the study.

The butler said wait here. Tom will be coming soon your mother too.

Tom and I sat not saying a word.

4575 Then in walked Tom senior and wife.

 Tom Jr parents

They took a long look at Tommy.

 In a few minutes looked at each other and said he could pass for Tom's and Joseph

brother.

4580 Then Tom senior asks what your mother's name?

Tommy said Hazel Viola Donily.

They answered and said no we don't know her.

Then ask what your grandfather's name

Tommy answered Ore Donily or Donnelly

585 Then tom senior set up and said yes, your Grandfather was in Chicago got into a jam with ell Capone.

My god tom senior said then ore got away.

We all thought Capone killed him.

Then tommy told the story he heard as a young boy yes grandpa stole a box of cash

590 from a heavy weight fight Capone was promoting

Then tom senor said that was the Dempsey and tune wavy wait Campion ship fight.

Ca pone's man chased grandpa across the whole country.

Gram mother was pregnant with my mother.

595 Then somewhere near Powers lake North Dakota grandpa dropped her off at a ranch for her to have my mother.

That's where my mother was born.

600 Then grandpa went on to Alberta Canada and purses his farm and ranch.

Then returned to Powers Lake to bring Granma and my mother to Alberta Canada

Tom senior asks did Capone ever get ore Donnelly? No sir, he is still around pretty old.

605 Well he survived probably the only one ever Capone killed everyone that stole from him. Tommy answered ore told me it was untenable to stile from and Italian.

Tom senior smiling then changed the subject and said meet your blood cousin tom Jr then tom came and shook my hand then hugged be besides.

10 The whole family did the same.

Tommy was accepted into the family.

Then the butler yelled dinner is set ready when you are.

Tom senior said let's enjoy this with some of the best red wine and New York beef

15 steaks.

Then another cousin walked in.

Tom said tommy meet your other cousin.

Tommy stood up and looked at a powerful well-muscled man!

Joseph looked then said nice to meet your tommy then Joseph shook Tommy's hand,

4620　tommy said yes nice to meet you Joseph.
Man, Joseph tommy asked you're in great shape about the same size as tommy but big muscles everywhere legs to his bull neck.

Tom Jr told everyone
4625　Tommy thinks he is a snooker player he beat a lower-class hustler out of five hundred at polo's today.
Joseph said I know everyone around that place and everyone in New York.
tommy ask would you point them out for me, Joseph said I'll do better than that I'll take you and setup the game and put the money up if you can shoot.
4630
Tommy if you can really play snooker there some big buck in it in New York

Tom senior asked who taught you to play tommy.

4635　Tommy started telling them about bill marks and he was the one who gave me a list to go hustle polo billiards is on that list. Joseph said show me that list.

Tommy had it in his wallet and handed it to Joseph.
Joseph looked at the list and said man who ever gave this list put you Wright in the
4640　heaviest and best hustlers in the world.
Joseph asks how your father knew all this

Tommy said again it was my Dad bill marks he was the champion Diamond Brady (hottest stick) in the year 1933 he was the champion here and in Baltimore.
4645　OK Joseph said I'll check that name out, Billy marks tommy said again.

OK Tom senior told Joseph and tom Jr to watch out for our little country cousin these hustlers will take everything from him.
Joseph said I'll take you around and find out just how good you can shoot.
4650
Tommy then said no Joseph you're not blowing my cover for free.
Just let me find my own way you will maybe hear latter.
OK Joseph said everyone knows me your right.

4655　Tom senior told the butler herald to take tommy and his bag to the small guest house and make sure he has everything.

Then tom Senior told tommy you can come and go as much as you need.

We will invite you for supper once a week.

Tom Jr or Joseph will take you around when he gets time.
OK tommy nice to meet you. First set we will have supper. It was great the Donnelly's treated me like family.
Then out the door old Harold took me with a late-night snack
65   Harold then told tommy doesn't come over to the main equators on till your invited tommy but you can ring me in the guest house if you need anything.
 OK tommy said' thanks
After herald left
 Tommy had a shower and laid down tommy was accosted.
70 It was quite a nice evening they knew my grandpa and told me about ell Capone trying to kill him.
And the small guest house was nice very classy
Tommy started thinking man I am a long way from Alberta Canada and feels like I am at home.
75 Tommy really was accepted tommy had real family in New York but they sure were mafia Tommy had to do thing right maybe do things by himself.

In the next few days' tommy learned a lot more about his new family.

80 Joseph was a fighter street fighter he would fight anyone for money his nick name was (The excellence of execution)
And tom Jr. was an astute businessman and tom Senior was the Head the Irish mafia national.
PLUS, THEY WERE ALL WHITE RABITS. (Meaning special agent status)
85 Very disguised and the highest status in the Irish organizations
Meaning CIA around the world contacts
Tommy liked what he seen thinking they just might come in handy someday.

 But I half to handle my own hustle or business I can do it myself.
90 Besides having Tom or Joseph with me would fuck up the whole thing.

Tommy stayed away from the main house,
Tommy rested up from the train and bus across America for two days.

4695 Then took the diamond Brady Queue and the old scratch up Queue he had from Spokane to play with until tommy got into a big money match then switch to the magic diamond Brady.
Tommy didn't know where to go in New York except polo billiards.

4700 tommy walked into polo's this time he was welcomed by the not so friendly bar tender the last time and would tell tommy whatever he wants we look after you he said OK tommy said please tell me witch hustler will be carrying cash.

The bartender said come to the bar.
4705 Then the bartender told tommy there are two good hustlers on the back two tables watch out there very good at the hustler's game tommy.

Tommy then said thanks and through the bartender a big twenty.

4710 Then walked slowly to the back table and set on the bench and watched both take money from some suckers.
The bartender was right both of them were experts. After they cleaned out their suckers
They both looked at tommy and said what you are looking at.
4715

Tommy smiled and said I think both of you are very good at this game.
They both looked at the country boy and said can you play if you can take your pick and challenge one of us.
Tommy said I'll try the one that was doing all the talking for Five dollars OK sir
4720

The one hustler said I know if he doesn't have any money and walked away.

The hustler answered well I don't play for five dollars.
The cheapest I play for is fifty dollars.
4725 Tommy said I'll play one game for fifty that's all the money I have.

Tommy won the first game then said I have one hundred now do you want to play for it.
Yes, he said.
4730 Tommy cleaned him out of fifteen hundred before he quit and said you're the luckiest

mother fucker I ever seen then walk out of polo's.

The bar tender just got off the phone to Joseph Donnell y and told him what he just witnessed.

35   The bartender then told Tommy you just cleaned one of the best in polo's Manhattan.

Tommy stayed around polos for a couple hours' no one came in to play.
 As he was setting at the bar the bartender told Tommy of one of the best high-class billiard halls in New York
40   It is called (GOLD FINGERS) it's over in queens.

 It's a classy new four-story building; the first floor is all rock and roll.
The second floor is hip hop music.
And the third floor is your style (country music)
45   But what you're interested in is the fourth balcony. it's the classiest billiard hall in America. You can't go there dressed like that. You at least must have a suit coat on to get in and a twenty-dollar cover charge.

All the players get anything they need. There are name players here.
50   I don't think you should go there...they we'll clean you out. It's a world class billiard hall and class of snooker players.
Tommy said please can you give me that address.
The bartender opened the phone book and wrote the address down.
 It's in Queens and 72 street.
55   Tommy said thanks Mr. and walked back to the mansion to have some supper. The butler Harold, always left a heaping dish for when I got home.
Then Tommy went to bed really thinking of how hard Gold Fingers would be
 The next night,
First Tommy had to go buy a suit jacket and I am going to get a tuxedo.
60

THE DONNELY MEETING ABOUT THIER NEW RELITIVE TOMMY MARKS Donily

Tom senior called Joseph and Tom Jr in for a meeting.
65   They were at the breakfast table tom senor said well we must find out all about Tommy and his Dad William Marks.

Then Tom said uses your contacts and find out if Tommy can shoot snooker and most important find out about his father Bill Marks. IF THAT WAS A TRUE STORY TOMMY TOLD US ABOUT HIS FATHER BEING THE CHAMPION IN 1933.

4770

We already know about this mother's side Mr. Ore Donily,
 He changed his name from Donnelly to Donily- thinking it would help him escape Capone.
Who chased Ore all the way to western Canada back in the years of the dirty thirties?

4775   We all thought Capone killed Ore, but I guess he didn't.

They both said yes, we would like to know too because it's strange Tommy showed up here like he did.
 Maybe he is telling the Truth Tommy said his dad gave him a list of places to go hustle

4780   and make a name for himself.
 They all smiled and said it won't take long to get all this info maybe three days.

Tom senor said we have a good pool player in the family Pete Crusher.

4785   He could find out all about if Tommy ever won any big tournaments or even beat any notables.
 Yes, Joseph said I have Pete's phone number I'll get him on that right away. Tom then asked to find out quick.
 Joseph said three days' tops.

4790

And I think Tommy had a dream or something it doesn't sound right.
 But Tommy already beat some good player's Tom senor agreed then said OK let's eat.

4795

Chapter- 20-the fight
(Excellence of Execution) "Joseph Donnelly"

Tommy woke up around eleven.
Showered, and then went jogging.

Tommy could not stop thinking about Gold fingers and the entire snooty world class billiard player walking around in their fancy cloths thinking they are the best.

well tommy is going to put the street hustle on the elite going to be interesting how they handle the real world.

The butler Harold said hey tommy come we are all going over to Howard Beach.
Joseph fights today.
Its big Tommy it's the champion street fight of the east coast.
And Joseph is not the favorite.
Joseph is an under Dog,
if he wins the odds against him are ten to one.
He is fighting a big Italian that destroyed everyone in seconds. Tom senior didn't want Joseph to fight this big ape.
Be ready in ten minutes and ride in the limo with tom and Joseph.
OK tommy said I am ready right now nobody told me about this fight.

Tommy was surprised Joseph could get hurt Howard BEACH it's the home of the "NEW YORK ITALIAN MAFIA"
The whole crowd was to meet under an old bridge that was half tore down on the water front. The Irish and the Italian mafias all (packing) and willing to bet anything on their boy.
There was only one street into Howard beach and no other way out, and it was governed by the Italians mafia.
On one side, there was the New York subway and on the other side it was an eight-lane freeway.
Then the other side all water Atlantic Ocean. Many gangsters tried to swim with

cement shoes.
Tom told me the bodies were never found in New York because the water would give the bodies a free ride to New Jersey that's out of state.

4835

 This was the Italians home as were on their turf.
There was two big strong man with their heaters, stopped every car only Irish or their Italian brothers allowed.

4840   Tom senior opened his window one inch at the entrance,
the Italians seen him and never said anything just opened the pipe barrier quickly.

Under the old bridge is where the fight would take place in just a few minutes.

4845   In the limo Joseph was calm. as if nothing was bothering him.

Tommy was scared just setting there nervous as hell tommy always sense danger.

This was an important fight who ever won it sets kind of seniority.

4850

There were around three hundred respected members of the Italian mafia standing around on their side with their mouths running.
As if there was a line drew all telling the Irish what's the matter you scared to bet "ha ha". Wanting to bet more on their man all packing heaters

4855   I know the Irish always packed two.
This looked like a dangerous place for tommy, I was looking for a quick way out of their it looked like the only place to run was the Atlantic.
Fuck tommy said I wish I never came?

4860   The Irish on the opposite sides all armed protecting their brand.
 Tom senior was going to shut the Italians mouth. Tom opened the window and sent an Irish heavy and taking advantage of Joseph's 10 to 1 underdog status. -

Tom Bet another $20.000.00 cash on Joseph.
4865   The Italian at the table nodded that meaning it was on. If Joseph won tom senior would pick up $200.000
 Joseph and the Italian champion both came out on their side looking at each other this stirred things up, the men on both sides started yelling.

The excitement was high.

370 Tommy looked at both men, the Italian man was much bigger and looked like he would destroy Joseph.

His eyes were on fire and the giant couldn't wait to grab Joseph and crash him.

Joseph said Tommy and smirked coldly and said I have plans for him this is for the east coast Championship-Watch and you will see.

'75

Tommy could feel the confidence in Joseph and the fear!

Joseph was the bravest man I ever seen.

If that big ape was looking at me like he was at Joseph I would be looking for a way out of here!

80 There were two tables where the Italians were taking bets.

The prize money was pilled at the end of the one table with a six-foot-long iron wait on top of over. $400.000.00 to the winner plus the side bets.

Every Irish and Italian bar in New York was taking action on the fight too!

85 This was a big fight.

The two-fighters walked close (eye to eye) It looked like the giant Italian would destroy Joseph.

Joseph was warming up stretching now, Joseph had a worried look his eyes almost looked deadly.

90 The big Italian when both fighters came close towered over Joseph.

Both mobs were yelling you could feel the electricity in the air this was fucking serious.

Joseph looked worried as they were about to rumble.

A gunshot rings out the fight was on!

95

THE FIRST MOVE THE ITALIAN RUSHED TOWARDS JOSEPH AND LANDED A glancing RIGHT TO JOSEPH'S JAW knocking Joseph to the pavement hard!

JOSEPH SPRANG UP TO HIS FEET and JUST BARELY GOT OUT OF THE WAY OF THE BIG
00 THUGS REACH.

It didn't hurt Joseph.

JOSEPH then CIRCLED THE BIG ITALIAN KEEPING HIM OFF BALANCE.

THE BIG ITALIAN WAS SWINING WILDLY AND FAST trying to kill Joseph.

05 JOSEPH KEPT CIRCLING TO HIS LEFT KEEPING THE BIG Italian OFF BALANCE HE COULD

NOT CONECT WITH JOSEPH CIRCLING to the left it kept him off balance.

JOSEPH LET THE THUG CHASE HIM For at least five minutes or more then Joseph punched him in the side of his head and that made the big man mad and he chased
4910 Joseph around and around the big Italian was starting to breath hard his mouth was open

JOESPH then pulled off a move no one ever seen before.
This was a new move.
4915 AS THE ITALIAN CHARGED JOSEPH
Which JOSEPH KNEW HE WOULD?
JOSEPH LITTERLY TURNED HIS BACK ON THE ITALIAN?

LOOKED LIKE JOSEPH WAS giving up.
4920 THE ILAILIAN CHARGED but JUST BEFORE THE ITALIAN WAS TO GRAB AND CRUSH JOSEPH,
JOSEPH SPRANG ON HIS HANDS THAN AT THE SAME TIME WITH BOTH LEGS KICKED THE BIG MAN STRIGHT INTO HIS RIBS with perfect timing.
THE Italian was rushing in and the force of josephs kick,
4925 THE BIG ITALIAN FELL TO THE PAVEMENT hard and was limp.
IT WAS OVER THE ITALIAN WAS OUT/
THE DOCTOR ran to him quickly started to EXAMINE THE ITALIAN HE WAS FINISHED.

HIS Ribs WERE DROVE INTO His LUNGS AND HEART.
4930 It was a deadly move.
THE DOCTOR was telling everyone this is serious get out of the way he might die,
then the doctor told the I TALIAN boys hurry they loaded the big man into the ambulance quickly the doctor went with the Italian in the ambulance told the Italian boss he might die.
4935 THE WHOLE CROWD WAS STUNDED.
THE IRISH WASTED NO TIME COLLECTING. JOSEPH $600, 000, 00 cash off the Italian table.

MAN, FOR A FEW MINUATES IT WAS TENCE/
4940 THE TWO ORGANIZATIONS HAD BAD BLOOD. THERE WERE LOTS OF BAD EYES the Irish were ready to start blasting.
THE Irish AGAINST THE ITALIANS ON THERE TURF.

THE HEAD OF THE ITALIANS Walked in between and SAID TAKE THE MONEY BUT WE
WILL BE GETING THAT BACK.WITH INTEREST FUCK YOU WHITE Rabbit.

045   Go back to hell's kitchen.
Joseph had white rabbit status I could see why holly fucks.

THEN WE DROVE OUT of HOWARD BEACH.
TOMMYS HEART WAS STILL BEATING FAST NO one was SAYING ANYTHING complete
050   silence.
TOMMY BROKE THE SILENCE AND SAID MAN I CAN SEE WHY THEY Call YOU
(THE EXCELENCE OF EXACAUTION)

NO ONE ANWSERED
055   The limo stayed silent all the way back to Manhattan.

When the limo entered the mansion tom senior told the mafia guard to close that
front gate and lock it post thirty men all around the estate now the guard quickly was
calling.
060
Then we parked in front of the main house, everyone got out and started to walk in
tom senor stopped and told Tommy to go to the guest house and don't go out for the
next four days or we tell you there could be a war.

065   OK Tommy answered.
Then tom senor told the gate boss that if that Italian fighter dies this could start a war.

The gate boss said I'll close things.
And get the word out quickly.
070   Tommy went to the guest house and stayed there turned on the TV on a love story.

The butler brought food and even herald was packing.
Three days later Joseph came and told Tommy that everything is now ok.

075   Tommy was sure glad of that he was getting restless.
First thing Tommy went out to polos for coffee (And relaxed)

CHAPTER 21-
Pete crusher New York Irish hustler

Mr. Pet crusher's investigation on Tommy and his father bill marks.

In the living room tom senor, tom Jr. and Joseph were looking at Pete crusher waiting for his report anxiously.

Well my investigation is finished.

Tom senor said let's hear it.

Well Tommy's Dad, Tommy story probably is true William Marks was a deadly hustler back in the year of 1929 in Vancouver Canada he showed up shooting a lame game.

Set everyone up nobody heard of him then he completely cleaned everyone out within two days, before the word could get around.

That's true.

Then he traveled by train to Chicago then New York then Baltimore where he beat the best in the world he was crowed the king diamond Brady in the year of 1933.thats true.

(NOW COMES THE IMPORTANT PART OF THE FAMILY STORY.)

Pete announced and was smiling while he was talking.

Tommy showed up at Spokane Washington and accidentally ran into one of the best hustlers in USA traveling through Spokane just to pick up some easy cash,

His name is Seattle slim. Tommy never knows who was slim.

Yes, tom senior said we watched him play lots in the Vegas championship tour!

Yes, Pete said according to slim I talked to him by phone.

Tommy took $50.000.00 dollars from him.

Slim say's Tommy has the nicest and smoothest country boy simile.

But it's really a shit eating grin and he plays so boring he puts you too sleep with his slow moves and fucking aggravating style.

It's all his game.
 That little bastard he did it to me.
015 I would never play him again anywhere fuck that little prick.
 I still have that little bastard in my mind when I try to sleep and I am upset all the time.
 Tommy fucking duped me I Mean THE COWBOY CONN MAN.
 "Slim said Please tell me somebody broke that little prick"

020 PET CRUSHER THEN SAID SOUNDS LIKE TOMMY IS A SLICK LITTLE BASTARD.
 AND A NOBODY IN THE BILLARD WORLD

 Joseph said if what you're telling us is there just might be an opportunity to steel some
 big buck with him.
025 If tommy is real or just got lucky beating slim?
 Well tom senor said sounds like Tommy is telling us the truth.

 Well Joseph said Tommy only told us his Dad gave him a list of places to go to.
 To make money Tommy never ever said he was a fucking hustler.
30 Tommy is always short of info Pete crusher said.
 Well tom senior said Tommy never lied.
 No but Tommy never told us he was a hustler.
 Tom senor smiles and said would you Joseph!!

35 Then tom senor asked Pete to do you think Tommy can beat the New York players.
 Pete answered well settle slim sure can when he is on.
 OK tom senor said no one say a fucking word about Tommy let's test him somehow.
 Pete, you get to be friends with Tommy and by accident get a named New York played
 to hustler Tommy in secrete.
40

 Tom senior then told butler Harold Give Pete a couple grand to spend time with
 Tommy now Pete report back every day or week I want to know what your opinion is.

 Pete said I'll play him if he beats me I can tell if he can play with the best in New York.
45 OK tom senior go play tommy but set tommy up be friends first,
 Be Tommy's guide showing him New York and make sure Tommy doesn't get into any
 trouble.
 And you try a beat him first.
 Pete said I'll have to play Tommy for money that's the only way we'll I know.

5050 Sounds like tommy only shoots when the moneys right

Pete crusher had an assignment.

And answered most hustler don't shoot unless there's money up that's how to tell bet. him.

Pete answered think I can clean Tommy out myself.

5055 OK tom said let us know how you and the New York hustler made out after that we will match Tommy for real money.

If tommy is good enough we could make a fucking fort ion?

Tommy was on his way to gold fingers to watch the big timers.

Tommy never took his Queue; this was to watch the players.

5060 Paid at the entrance as a spectator

Tommy walked into the fancy room bleachers all around the gigantic room.

There were eighteen billiard tables in a half moon theater two were set up with cameras.

5065 Tommy watched all the players and their styles there was one that was the best by far he was a slim well-dressed Italian Slicker with not a hair out of place black greasy Italian

The announcer introduced him his name was (Stanley sting) was shooting like a champion and was showing off with a few trick shots.

5070

Nobody could warm him up Stanley sting was clearly the best at gold fingers there was a crowd following Mr. Sting he was the champion.

Tommy watched sting for around three hours (Italian Royalty.)

5075

Tommy noticed a couple things Mr. Sting might be week at and the most venerable was his (attitude) maybe a few insults would rock stings world?

Tommy thought it would be a hard hustle Mr. Sting shot to good.

5080 Tommy decided to stay away from Stanley sting it would be too hard to gamble or try and hustle Mr. Sting.

Then tommy returned to the Donnell y mansion in deep thought maybe New York would be too hard.

5085 Tommy was thinking of moving out of New York?

Tommy just entered the guest house and in walked Joseph.
 Hi tommy Joseph said tommy replied with how are you any sore spots.
Joseph answered nope.
090   Then Joseph said I have a friend with Joseph then introduced Pete Crusher to tommy.

Joseph told tommy pet will take you around New York, show you all the hot spots other than old polo's billiards and Pete is a good billiard player too tommy.

095   Tommy shook hands with Pete and said when we can start seeing New York.

Pete said let's go right now bring you stick you mean shoot some yes Pete said.

Tommy went to the guess house and walked over to the bed and pick up the Diamond
00   Brady Queue and said OK Mr. crusher let's see New York.
Pet took tommy to an old pool hall in Queens called mayflowers.

Then Pete couldn't wait to clean tommy out and send him back to the farm.

05   Pet looked at tommy like he was a punk.

And in the car, he never talked.
Pet was going to make fast work of this country boy.

10   Pete racked the balls, never said a word flopped five hundred cash in the top right corner pocket.
Told tommy to match the five hundred and then said break them.
Tommy answered what is this, are you trying to scare me.
 Pete said you're going to be leaving NEW YORK quickly kid.
15   Tommy said well I guess we will see tommy matched the five hundred and said I thought we were supposing to be friends. Pete just looked coldly.

Tommy broke the balls fluke one red then tommy ran thirty points then played a safety leaving Pete nothing.
20   Pete tried to leave a safety but missed then tommy ran the table.

THE FIRST GAME WAS EASY WIN FOR TOMMY.
Then Pete said you fucking lucky bastard.

Then through fifteen hundred in the top right pocket

5125   Tommy figured out this fucking New York hustler was trying to break tommy and send him home.

Pete said matches it and that was all he said we weren't friends.

This was a very unfriendly match.

5130   You could see Pete hated tommy or was jealous of what he heard from Seattle slim.

Tommy matched the $1500.00

This game went the same way tommy took two thousand bucks from Mr. Crusher.

In only two games Pete said let's go.

5135   Pete drove tommy back to the Donnelly mansion never said a word.

Just get out! When we arrived

Tommy got out shut the car door and walked into the guest house.

5140   Joseph was working out in the yard seen tommy carting his pool Que.

Joseph asked where you just came from

Your supposed to be looking at New York with Mr. Crusher

Tommy said oh that ignorant little guy you introduced to me wanted to clean me out

5145   and send me home to the ranch.

Well what happened Joseph asked?

He lost only two games and I cleaned him out.

5150   Joseph asked how much did you win from Pete.

Tommy answered only two thousand he never had much to lose.

Joseph looked and said you only left an hour ago.

Then said I have to go to the house see you tomorrow tommy.

5155   Joseph went into the study and told Tom senior you gave Pete two thousand dollars

less than an hour ago well Pete lost it to tommy.

Tommy just cleaned Pete out

In only two games

Tommy won that two thousand you just gave to Pete.

5160   Tommy has your cash already"

Tommy took it quickly!

Tom senor said we will talk to Pete about it Pete might be setting Tommy up.

OK Joseph said you think Tommy will crack if he is under pressure.

Tom said again let's call Pete!

65

But if Pete lost that two thousand that fast only around and hour it doesn't look good for Pete.

Maybe Tommy can shoot tom said.

Joseph started dialing Pete

70 Pete answered Joseph asked how you and tommy get along

Pete said yes that country fuck nailed me.

Joseph said what happen.

Then Pete said if I ever get a chance to fuck that sneaky bastard I'll do it fast.

Why are you so mad Pete' Joseph asked'?

75

Pete then said that dirty fucker he leaves the Queue ball laying along the fucking rail or snuggled up to another ball where I can't see any balls and every fucking time too.

He can't shoot that good but plays and asshole game classless!

Fucking bastard

80 That country fuck is the most aggravating dirty fucking bastard just like Seattle slim said and he never say's a word it's the look on his face a fucking grin as if he is enjoying it all with not a care in the world fuck that bothers me. Slim said his handle is

(The Cowboy con man)

Joseph said OK Pete you can stay away from him then.

85 Tommy is so polite around us.

Pete said try and play snooker with that mother fucker. Pete said I bet him 1500 all at ones tried to shake him up it never bothered him one little bit.

Thanks Joseph crusher said I never want to see him that aggravating bastard again the

90 conversation was over.

Joseph looked at tom senor and said Tommy is for real but let's watches a little more if he beats another good New York class shooter player then we'll get on Tommy's side.

95 But one thing Pete is sure finished.

And Tommy got to him big time even broke pet's heart it sounds like.

Joseph said to tom senor it only took Tommy one hour to get your two thousand Tom's.

5200 Tom senor started smiling best investment I made in a while smiled tommy has our attention no

CHAPTER 22-

Irish protection & INCOME over $270.000.000 million per year

5205 Joseph now was interested in talking to the new cousin; Joseph woke Tommy up and asked Tommy if he would ride around the city with him today.

Tommy jumped out of bed and answered yes Joseph give me five for a shower.
OK Joseph said I'll wait at the car.

5210 Tommy came out of the guest house fresh then Joseph drove out and went towards main Manhattan.
Stop in front of a skyscraper. And said watch the car. And went into the building this went on all day every time Joseph walk out of a skyscraper he had sometimes a bag, other times a box locked them in the trunk and drove to another.

5215
Tommy knows what it was in the boxes or bags it was protection money.

Then over too queens same thing there
This went on all day.

5220 Then some stops at movie studios.

Then the wharf ware all the cargo ships were unloading and loading that took the rest of the day.
Joseph told Tommy if he could beat one of the best name players they could put

5225 something real big to gather.
Tommy said like what Joseph.
Well Joseph said we are fight promoters boxing; we could put a snooker match together.
Big bucks Tommy but you have to stop that hustling game and start just shooting

5230 Joseph said and looked at tommy.
Tommy grinned, and then Joseph shook his head.

Can you do that Tommy?

Tommy answered I don't know I never did it before accepting when I played dad.

235   But what kind of money we are talking

Joseph said millions Tommy.

Tommy said now you're talking all I have to do is beat the best in New York.

Fuck those sharks over at gold fingers look fucking hard to beat.

I might not be able to beat any of them they look better than me.

240

Joseph said go try and see if you have a chance.

OK Tommy said I'll try and Gage their talent tommy was serious now.

This was the first time any of the Donnelly's spent any time with Tommy.

45

Tommy slept that night and jugged the next morning.

Then sleep and relaxed the whole day. On-till eight thirty at night.

50   Then washed his face then took the diamond Brady Queue out and wiped cleaner all over the Queue.

IT had to be ready for some real hard snooker.

Then walked to the street and held a cab. Tommy said please take me to gold fingers in
55   queen's sir. The driver said around twenty minutes.

Then when they were going over the bridge the driver said are you playing at gold fingers sir.

Tommy answered I never before this will be my first time.

60

The driver smiled and said maybe you better think that over son it's the best snooker players in the United States.

Then the driver said where you from son.

Tommy told him Alberta Canada.

65   Well I bet you return back to Canada very fast going to gold fingers.

Don't mean you any insult but you're heading in to the fires of hell of snooker players.

I know of away easier places to go.

Do you want me to take you there, the cab driver knows everything?

Tommy said no thanks take me to the hungry lions. The cab driver said OK Mr.

70

First test at Gold fingers

5275

GOLD FINGERS NEW YORK

Tommy entered gold fingers the billiard room was a three-quarter circle.
With glass between the seats and the tables
At the left side, there were the small players trying to get to the top.

5280

The rug was yellow that meant showing amateur's the yellow took forty per cent of the room.
Then there was green rug which indicated sharks.

5285   But the last two tables the rug was bright red.
With waiters and referrers racking the ball with white gloves on that is where the gold fingers book makers and cameras.

Tommy entered the yellow amateur tables the first player the bet was one hundred

5290   Put in the front pocket Tommy was not hustling now.

Tommy listened too Joseph Tommy made a quick victory. then moved up but still on the yellow rug.
The bet was two hundred; Tommy made a short game victory.

Then Tommy moved to the green rug, the bet started at five hundred.

Tommy had a little harder game but pulled the win off.

Tommy moved higher up still on the greed rug.

The same bet five hundred. The games were getting harder but Tommy got another win.

Tommy never knew that Pete Crusher was in the sets watching hoping tommy would get his ass kicked.

Tommy won again and moved to the first table in the red rug zone.

And there was the Italian slicker. Stanley sting, first thing that came out of his mouth was the bet is twenty-five hundred.

Pete crusher phoned Joseph and told Joseph what was happening Pete told Joseph that Tommy just got through the sharks in the green now tommy is at the table in the red zone. Now tommy is challenging Stanley sting for twenty-five hundred.

Tommy looked at the dress style of the Italian slicker, with a cat greasy mu stash with a slick black vest and smiling like –I got you.

Pet told Joseph tommy is fucked now.

Pet said Mr. Stanley sting. There making the bet now cash is in the top left pocket.

Joseph said stay on the phone, tell me what's happening.

Tommy Broke and played a safety sting can't see a ball.

Sting tried to make a long shot and missed going for the table.

Tommy ran sixty points then hocked sting tight again.

Sting could not see a ball.

Sting mist again

Then Tommy ran the table out.

Pete told Joseph tommy just Beat sting easily Pete said tommy won easy.

Joseph was excited and was asking how that happened Pete did.

"Pete said holly fuck Tommy just beat Mr. Sting fucking easy.

What Joseph said impossible till me how (fuck?)
Pet said tommy and sting are going to bet ten thousand now.
Tommy is counting his cash out.

5335

"Pete, you get those two friends of yours and get Tommy out of there right fucking now before the next game no more games that's a fucking order!

Yes, Sir Joseph Pete motioned to the Irish heaves

5340

Remove Tommy from gold fingers now Pete don't fuck around Joseph was stern

Stanley sting was mad at Tommy but was emptying his pockets and talking big time shit to tommy.

5345   Pete and two Irish mafia heavies entered the red zone

Saying come Tommy its over Pete told Tommy Joseph said it's over.

"Tommy told Pete I don't take orders from Joseph"

5350

Pete told sting Tommy is out of here (sting said we are just starting)

That punk walks in there and challenges me.
And now you are taking him out.

5355

I want to know who this punk
Sting was mad demanded who is this ignorant punk.

As they were walking out the door Tommy yelled I am a street hustler they call me
5360   (The cowboy con man)
Sting said who the cowboy con man
Pete answered yes something like (only street hustler)

Then out the door we went.
5365   Tommy said why Joseph did this
"Pete was Tommy's friend now"
And replied Tommy listen to Joseph he has bigger things coming
You just proved yourself you beat sting and it looked easy.

But sting might have been setting you up.

370

Pete said Please Tommy listens to Joseph.
Pet crusher had a different sound in his voice now.

Pete said Stanley sting was mad

375

Tommy that means something

Tommy Said I only got him for twenty-five hundred but I had a good night I made a little over four thousand.

380

Pete said it wasn't the money tommy.
You showed sting you could beat him;
 No one ever came in especially a stranger unknown off the street and jerked him like that.

85 Tommy said yes, he sure was mad!
I can still see that grease mustache flopping as he was ruining his mouth.
We drove into the Manhattan mansion;
Joseph was waiting and waved us inside.

90 Straight into the den Joseph then said Tommy we might be able to put something together for you do you think you can defeat Mr. Sting in a four out of seven game.

Or do you think sting was setting you up.

95 Tommy said I don't know for sure.
 I wasn't hustling any more tommy was going to win and Stanley sting never even got a shot I handled sting this time and I think I had sting on the ropes.
This is just my feelings.
 It might be different in the next game.

00 Tommy said I sure would like to try Mr. Sting.
Joseph started asking Pete.
What do you think about a match with tommy and Mr. Sting meaning what kind of odds will tommy have?
Pete answered big odds Joseph;

05 Sting is the best in New York with many champion ships under his belt nobody will

challenge him.

Tommy has not won anything except being a fucking back ally hustler.

5410 But tommy is one of the best I ever seen he beat Seattle slim out of fifty Grande.
Joseph then asked how Seattle would slim measure up to sting.

Well Pete said if Seattle slim is on and again slim won Meany championships too.
5415 It probably would be a good match for sting.

Plus, this never happened in history, A street hustler competing against a world class champion like Mr. Sting.

5420 The odds would be at least one hundred to one against tommy.
Well Joseph said thanks for finding everything out Pete.
No problem Joseph Pete said

Let me think about this for the night good night.
5425 Out the door we went.
Tommy went to the guess house.

The next morning Joseph came to the guest house and asked Tommy please do not play any more snooker in public.
5430

Pete will look after you travel with you train you for maybe I can arrange a match.

I am going to start talking and we will see what comes out of it?

5435 Listen to Pete.
Joseph said I am going to challenge the people who back Stanley sting so stay away from any hustling in public.
OK Tommy said Let's put something big together I am ready for it.

5440 "Joseph then added and keep your big mouth shut don't talk about it to nobody just relax. .

Tommy said yep I will but that will be hard because I am beginning to not like Mr. Stanley sting,

145   he is ignorant self-centered ass hole and Italian besides.

Joseph said Tommy Mr. sting is a champion snooker player, tommy you haven't even entered that class yet.

150

 The only reason we'll back you is there will be at least one hundred to one against you.

Sting has the advantage in every category Tommy!

155 Tommy answered I don't think so Pete I know I can defeat him inside because I can feel it.
(Pete said people suffer from heart break thinking that way)
You are fucking show me some talent, no more built in Governor Start shooting.
Stop thinking of ways to take my money just shoot you're in big shit tommy.
160 Pete said I am here to get you as ready as I can
Tommy start listening to me Pete was saying.

 The Irish are getting the best odds and a lot of money on you.
Tommy looked and though for a few seconds then answered yes Pete your right this is
165 not a hustle. But what's tommy per cent age The Cowboy Needs to know.
OK tommy said it's on I'll listen to you except some advice.

70

75

5480

5485

Mr. Slick

Stanley sting without the cat muse ash
The Italian slicker king of New York forcing the cowboy con man's hand it's all presser!
5490 Tommy wanted or needed some (time along;
The water was close by a few blocks away.

Tommy walked to the shore the Manhattan Beach.
There he found the beach empty it was nice there was an old drift log washed up and
5495 that's where tommy set quiet listening to the sounds of New York City it was alive.

Then big cargo ships blowing their steam Horns.

Tommy's mind went back to the ranch in Alberta Canada and Mom and Dad.
5500 It was a breath of reality tommy dreadfully deeded;
Tommy was so far from that great way of life.

With nothing but real people just trying to get by with the harsh winters and hot dry
summers.
5505 (Tommy missed it)

But it was home and New York is so big people cold hearted.
New York was another world.

CHAPTER 23
JOSEPH'S SET UP THE
Italian mafia plus everyone in New York (BY ACSEDENT)

Tommy set around the guest house all day. Then Pete comes and they would go out for supper in nice restaurants away from any action.

Pete then would take tommy across the tunnel under the Hudson River to a nice small billiard hall in New Jersey
We shot latest 10 games.
Pet winning most of them.
Tommy was enjoying Pete's company after training with a cold Milwaukee beer.

Then tommy asked Pete why you don't want to play for a little cash it would make things more interesting. Pete you're winning most of the games.

Pete said I am here to make you aware of a couple of thing you do wrong.

But Tommy I know if I bet two cents everything changes.

Tommy, you have been Hustling for so long you have a built in Governor inside you.

You have to now stop that and shoot real fucking pool.
 Like you did that first night at Gold Fingers Stanley sting is coming after you and you're hustling. (Tommy wake up)
Pete was telling Tommy.
You're going to have to play the best you can and then some!

To defeat sting, he will be gunning for you.
You're the only guy that walk into Gold fingers and beat sting off the street.
You're called a fucking street hustler and should have never even been there at all.

5540 So, start shooting play your safety shots get those shots down perfect you're going to need them to slow sting down.
And I notice you're hesitant on some long shots.

Pete said I am going to take you to the best in New York eye's doctor he will check your
5545 eyes and fit you with enhanced eye sight.

Then you have to learn to shoot with glasses.

Tommy tomorrow I'll take you to see Dr Pearl eye specialist his office is on eighty
5550 second across from central park.
Then tomorrow night no more Governor you are fucking shooting Tommy.

The next night Joseph came to the guest house and talked to Tommy.

5555 Joseph said well Tommy we have a deal with the Italian boys.

You and Mr. Stanley sting are on you are in the biggest match up of your life.

The off-track betting of New York will carry the fight.
5560 You mean the snooker match;
Tommy asks what the money look like Joseph

Joseph said it's always about the money with you Tommy,"

5565 Joseph smiled.
Then said the odds are starting at fifty to one on you.
sting is a big favorite.
The odds might go to hundred to one we will let the off-track betting set the odds.

5570 Tommy, you train with Pete.
And beat him get as sharp as you can.
You got two weeks.
The bookies will set odds every day.
Probably there will be too much money comes in on sting.
5575 They think you are a flash in the pan.

Joseph said Tommy,
 you will never be able to hustle anymore after this match, especially if you win.

580   Tommy said OK no more governors on I'll shoot.
       Pete came then we drove over to Dr Pearl

       The examination showed Tommy tear duck in the left eye was excreting more liquid
       than needed.
585   Dr Pearl said Tommy eyes are very good but the liquid makes it harder for him to see
       perfect under presser.
        But I can improve his eye site by 20% with shooting glass's his eyes will improve to the
       best possible.

590   Tommy don't use these glasses for reading or driving

       Just when you shoot professionally Dr Pearl told tommy

       OK doc Tommy said I can't wait to try those new glasses out.
595

       Dr Peal said pick them up tomorrow at one.

       Then Pete and Tommy went to a privet Irish club where the public was not interfering.
       It was different Tommy now dominated.
600

       Tommy won eight games strait.
       Pete said enough.
       I'll come tomorrow we'll get your glasses then train after.

05   The next day Pete picked up Tommy glasses.
       Then told Tommy to try them on do they fit
       Tommy said perfect there's elastic that fit around your head it holds the glass's perfect
       they won't move.
       Then Pete took Tommy to an Irish private club.
10   There were a few Irish there having a cold beer.
       Pete racked the balls. Tommy cracked them and ran the table Pete said you're ready as
       he put his queue away.
       Pete said no fucking way I am sick of you you're to fucking hot for this Irishman.

5615 The Irish boys heard Pete and started saying Pete we thought you were the ultimate champion and started poking fun at Pete.
Pete then said OK I'll show you what I am up against.

Tommy let's see how many racks you can run without missing a fucking shot
5620 Tommy broke the ball in the first exhibition.

Ran the whole table without missing a shot

Dr Pearl's glasses really helped even the long shots.
5625

Tommy was starting to shoot perfectly Tommy would shoot using English making the shot and bringing the Queue ball just about anywhere he wanted.

Tommy ran the second rack.
5630

Pete stated racking the third
the Irish boys left the bar stoles and came over to the pool table and watched as Tommy broke and ran the table seven times out of ten racks.

5635 Only missed one shot in the seven games.
Seven out of ten racks (AMAZING) without missing a shot.
Then Pete said what you think about that

The Irish boys in the bar ask who is this guy tell us his name.
5640 Joseph will be after you if you tell anyone boys,"

We know nothing will go out of this private Irish club it's Irish for a reason.
Pete said Tommy your fucking ready take some time off.
We have two weeks then I think," Mr. Sting is going to get a lesson from a country boy
5645 Tommy stay at home don't drink eat good food and jog every day. (Pete was happy)

Tommy said I'll be fucking ready for that grease ball.

Then Pete said bi for now call if you need anything.
5650 Tommy set in the guest house counting the cash he made in New York and the extra

amount of cash he could afford to lose.
 It came to over $50.000.00

Tommy walked over to the main house and there was Harold waiting at the door.
55   He was the butler and guard.
 He watched the camera, and meats tommy at the door.
 Greeted tommy then said do you want to see tom.
 yes, tommy replied.
 Come in and go to the study,
60   (I'll get tom)
  In a few minutes in came Mr. Tom smiling.
 What can I do for you tommy?
  Tommy then ask tom what are the odds on me to beat sting.

65   Tom said very hi tommy you're a street hustler you can't seem to lose that status.
 Tommy asks again.
  Tom looked at tommy and said why.
 Ok tommy said I'll call myself.
 Tom said don't you do that; we don't need you showing any interest betting.
70

 Ok tommy said I am betting how I can do it.
 Tom said your odds are against you.
  You never played anyone like Stanley sting,
  Tommy or never played anywhere.
75

  You're not that class yet.
 But we are trying to get you there.
 Tommy then laid it out first Mr. Tom with all respect.
  First, I am a fucking hustler and one of the best.
80   I know better than you or that want to be Pete crusher.

 If you don't place my bet, I will.

 Oh, for god sake tom senior said ok.
85   Tommy asked what the odds are right now.

 Tom senior told Harold to call and get the spread.

In five minutes Harold was back and gave tom the paper.

Well Tommy your setting at eighty to one underdog.

5690   Then toms ask what do you want to bet $500.

Then tommy pulled out the $10.000.00 cash and handed it the Tom senor.

Tom took the cash and ask are you that confident tommy.

Tommy answered no but you never know how good I am because I am always playing

5695   the hustling game.

 I want to go out with something to remember.

If I lose I am giving it my all.

OLD Tom smiled and took the money and said I'll get your bet on tonight tommy and

5700   good luck tommy we can't bet on you it's too risky Mr. sting is too good for you.

The next morning tom Senior told tommy. (The odds are now sixty too one) that's a

nice pay day tommy if you win that's $ 500.000 00 tommy It's done tommy.

Tom senior said.

5705   Tommy said thanks and good night sir.

Then tommy went back to the guest house

Tommy now was back to himself as the hustler's manipulation

s and gaining confidence every minute.

5710   And now was thinking of ways too hustler everyone and maybe get more money down.

 The family had things set up only to make a per cent age on all the money bet they

decided not to bet on tommy.

5715   Not backing tommy.

 Now I'll hustle all NEW YORK plus.

I now have to figure out how to bet more money without anyone knowing.

5720   I will stay away from the whole family this is big business now?

(Three-day latter)

Tommy heard of a two-bit hustler over in jersey his name was frank Skippy.

 He played at some casino there he lived on the black horse pike close to Atlantic City

725 tommy told Harold that tommy would be gone for a day or so.

Harold said ok I'll tell Joseph.

Never saying where or what tommy was up too.

730 Tommy got on the train to Atlantic City New Jersey it was a wonderful train ride thought New York City under the Hudson then through the vine grape wine country of jersey then tommy got a room in Atlantic City.
The first night scouted the snooker halls and finely found frank Skippy he was a Atlantic city small time hustler that tommy could set up and take everything he owned and ever

735 would own!
Tommy asks Mr. Skippy if he was up to a game or two.

Mr. Skippy looked at the shit eating country boy and smiled if you got a hundred sons.
Tommy answered yep I do.

40

The first game Mr. Skippy won easy.

Then Mr. Skippy said how much cash you got let's get this over with,
Tommy went through every pocket and came up with two hundred fifty dollars that's

45 all I have sir.
Skippy match it then Skippy broke the balls.

Never made a ball on the brake and left him open.

50 Then tommy shot some down then tommy then missed.
Mr. Skippy almost ran the rest but missed again
Tommy shot and missed again.

Then Mr. Skippy won the game.

55

Tommy was broke and acted sad Mr. Skippy asked what is your name son tommy said well they call me the cowboy con man?

Then the whole bunch started to laugh.

50 Then tommy asked would you please give me train fair back to New York City please.
Mr. frank Skippy.

Skippy said yes son
And handed tommy forty dollars

5765   Then Skippy told tommy please don't try and play snooker over there

Tommy said I am quitting this game it has keep me broke for years.

We'll remember your name it's the Cowboy Con Man.
5770

They shook their heads saying stupid. "He he"
Tommy did exactly what he wanted the word would be everywhere by tomorrow

As soon as they see the match in New York,
5775   The word will fly around;

CHAPTER 24

Even the family will lose their confidence when they hear about this. Small town hustler beats The Cowboy Con Man frank Skippy.
5780

Then I'll bet more when the odds go to one hundred to one.

Thank you, Mr. Skippy, and his friends will try and destroy the cowboy's reputation and bet thousand against the cowboy.
5785   Things are fucking starting to come together by accident.
Dad was right things will happen just play it right tommy (Dad would say)

On the way, back to Manhattan looking out of the train window at the city lights tommy was thinking of leaving New York it was nice the family was protecting but
5790   tommy felt controlled somehow.
Tommy never had anyone telling me anything

That was the style of life tommy had to feel free the country air freedom was now important.
5795   Tommy decided after the Stanley sting match.

Tommy is going back hustling but maybe not snooker.
Tommy was looking at the map Dad gave him, the list Brown town Delaware full of bookies Dad said, then the California inn in Marylyn

300

Tommy realized its only ninety-five miles south on highway 95 Delaware.

Seven days to wait then we will see if the cowboy can beat the New York finest Stanley sting.

305

I don't know but every time I am over matched I seem to like it.
Sting might make short work of me but inside me but there' always away I'll find something he doesn't like! I'll play him the cowboy way.

310   He will get frustrated or piss off something he isn't ousted too.

The train was get close to central station New York.

In one-day tommy was going to take another trip to visit brown town Delaware.

15

Dad knowns about things, dad said bookies were all over brown town Delaware.
Tommy sleeps the night and half the next day.

Then went jogging
20   Eat a New York steak and retired for a nice night sleep again.
The next day it was three days before the Stanley sting match.
Harold came to the guest house and told tommy Joseph wants to talk to him right now.

Tommy walked to the mention.
25   Harold gave both coffees.
Then Joseph started talking saying well tommy we aren't betting on the game we are taking a per cent age of the whole betting pool.

Tommy said that ok sting's going to win anyway.

30

Joseph said you have changed you mind tommy,
Tommy answered I just realized Stanley sting is for real.

Joseph said there are only three nights then it's on.

5835   The odds are up more now there almost sixty-five to one against you tommy. You have some followers.

Joseph said again we are not betting a thing but hope you do well tommy.

Tommy said thanks.

Then out the door back to the guest house.

5840

Now tommy had everything on his side.

That night tommy left the guest house around 3:30.in the morning.

Took a cab to central station central New York got on the flyer high speed rail to

5845   Baltimore but in stopped at wellington Delaware.

Brown town was just below the hill.

Part of Wilmington Delaware

Took a cab to the strip called brown town

5850   There was people everywhere the street was full.

Tommy walked into the first bookie joint on the strip.

It was full horse racing monitors showing horse racing in meadowlands, Belmont Park, Kentucky tracts. Philadelphia Park

5855

Plus, they were booking the Stanley sting snooker verses The Bar room hustler the cowboy con man.

Tommy went to the counter and asked what the odds on the cowboy con man in New York.

5860   The lady said sixty to one sir.

Tommy said I would like to place a bet please. Ok she started typing tell me who your betting and how much.

Tommy handed five thousand dollars and said the Cowboy con man.

She looked at the five thousand and said ho I should get permission for that amount.

5865

She scurried back then a man came warring a black suite.

The man said I am the manager.

Then we shook hands son he said who you are betting on. Tommy answered the

5870   cowboy con man sir I know him in Canada

Then the manager asked can I see some ID yes tommy placed his drivers Lic on the counter.
The manager looks at it and said ho you're from Canada
Tommy Marks (Take his bet) the manager told the lady.

75

That was easy the lady gave tommy an official ticket for five thousand dollars bet the odds were at sixty to one she said there a little profit we have to make son.

Tommy went to two more bookies it was no problem none of the bookie joints new the
80   name tommy marks.
Had anything to do with the cowboy con man
Just took the bets.
After a few drinks
Tommy was on his way back to New York in two hours' tommy had fifteen thousand
85   bets at sixty to one.
Plus, ten thousand at fifty to one in New York
Total bet was twenty-five thousand dollars.
If tommy could win the prize money and the gamble could reach total $1.700.000.00
All tommy had to do was beat the Italian slicker Stanley sting.
90

Tommy arrived back to central station in New York before midnight.
No one expected a thing; even the Delaware bookies never connected tommy and the Cowboy Con Man.
Now tommy had to focus on the game.
95   The bets were down,
Now Stanley sting.
Tommy was starting to hate that Italian mother fucker.

Tommy's perfect how can I fuck that bastard up.
00   We will meet just before the game the night before there is an interview live on closed circuit that's when I'll start.

Two days before the match Pete crusher came to the guest house to see tommy.

05   Pete said tommy you have been staying by yourself lately is there anything wrong.
No tommy said I am OK.

Well tom and Joseph want to see if you're ready for Mr. Sting

5910   They are waiting at the club to watch you train let's go give them a show tommy.

On the way to the club, tommy was seriously thanking?
Tommy is going to test how good of family I have.
When Pete and tommy walked into the Irish club Joseph greeted us first then tom
5915   senior.
Pete racked the balls tommy broke then missed, and then Pete almost ran the table.
Tommy missed again.
Then Pete won easily.
The second game everyone was watching, same kind of game tommy looked off.
5920   Pete said what's won again!
Tommy said I quit I can't concentrate.
In a few minutes Joseph came and said tommy what's wrong
Tommy said I am scared of Stanley sting I have a nervous problem.
THE IRISH CLAND looked stunned.
5925   Tommy knows he just lost the backing of all the Irish.
Witch was just what I wanted.
Pete was driving tommy back to the guest house not saying a word.
Stopped in front tommy got out of his car without saying a word.

5930   Tommy walked in through the main gate peeked back and seen Pete shaking his head
and saying chicken shit.
Tommy now knows all the Irish were going to bet on Stanley sting.
The Cowboy Con Mans odds would claim to over one hundred to one.
Tomorrow afternoon around five hours before the match tommy would bet another
5935   ten thousand, that would make my winnings well over $2.500.000.00 million.

Tommy sleep all night and most of the day.
Then took a cab to the Bronx went into their off-track parlor and place five thousand
on the counter showed his tommy marks Donily drivers Lic the clerk check took a photo
5940   of the Lic and gave it back with the ticket.

Not recognizing tommy as the cowboy con man.
No one new Tommy Marks Donily.
The same thing happened at off track parlor across from the meadowlands race track

on the New York side.
Tommy got the ten thousand bets without anyone knowing a thing.

Tommy jumped on the train back to Manhattan by the time tommy reached the mansion there was three hours before the match starting with the important live interview. Tommy cut some cucumbers up and placed them on both eyes.
And tried to get some rest

One hour before interview time Pete crusher woke tommy up and said get ready tommy it's almost time.
Tommy was already dressed in a working ranch straw cowboy hat on.

Well PETE said you really look like a hay seed with that hat on.

Then pet said why didn't you didn't tell us about your Atlantic City hustle with the cheap street hustler frank Skippy.
Tommy act surprised how you know about that.
Ho tommy we know Avery thing.
Their ok tommy we are going around to back door and betting

Mr. Sting so don't worry
Tommy said thank Pete like a little boy.

In the dressing room tommy opened the
(DIAMOND BRADY) the purple satires came alive then Tommy heart started feeling strong.
All the great champions' spirits were there!

Tommy could feel their presents
Tommy eyes and adrenalin was starting to flow Tommy ran his hand up and down over the purple satires;
They lit up like they know the challenge was on.

The referee opened Tommy's door and said there ready for the pre-match interview.
This was what tommy was waiting for a chance to piss off Mr. Sting.

Tommy was ready for that fucking greasy conceded Italian.

I can't stand the way his hair is
Not a hair out of place napkin folded up perfect.
I'll get to him big time that fuck isn't used to these he things he is class my ass!!!

5985

There sting was with not a hair out of place dressed in black with vest blue in front.
The announcer interviewed Mr. Sting not even looking at the COWBOY.

Sting was going on about his long championship and the announcer was agreeing.

5990

Finally, the announcer turned around and looked at the hay seed in the western hat.

And put on a funny smile and said well cowboy con man where was the last bar room
you played at smiling.

5995

Tommy smiled and said sir is you part of Mr. Sting's boy girl's partners.
Sting goes both ways.
What do you mean by that cowboy? (The arouser said abruptly) then the cowboy said
the word on the street where I come from

6000

Mr. Sting goes both ways but proffers man.
The announcer was stunned and took the microphone away from the cowboy.
Mr. Sting was so mad he started to push Tommy.

6005   The security both grabbed sting and held him back Sting was going to punch the
cowboy.
The look in stings eye's he was mad he was glaring at the cowboy.
Sting was upset.
The announcer was doing the same saying who to hell do you think you are.
6010   Then the security followed both back to our dressing rooms.

Tommy walked away yelling over his shoulder your man and wife.
They were both hot. Tommy was escorted to his room inside tommy started to laugh.
Now I have that greaser up set, I'll stay after him its working he just isn't used to a little
6015   conversation. Now Mr. Sting is in the cowboy's world I found out what bothered him!

BAR ROOM HUSTLER CALLED THE COWBOY CON MAN

GOLD FINGERS NEW YORK

20

The referee knocked on Tommy's door fifteen minutes' cowboy its game time and behave you.

Tommy held the diamond Brady queue that Dad won in 1929.

Tommy was waiting for the call.

25

Somehow inside tommy knows he could beat sting it was part of Tommy's destiny

The biggest pay day in Tommy's life

I'll take it to at Italian all night fucking night called trash talk on the street we call is shit talking.

30 Italians have a worse temper then the Irish.

They are just too high strung! Poor guys!

The door opened ok cowboy they want you to enter first.

Tommy took a deep breath then Tommy's attitude went to high

35

pumped himself up then walked out of the dressing room down the narrow hallway to a noisy crowd and the lights and cameras were straight on the cowboy walking to the snooker table there were three announcers that were all x champions.

40 The cowboy con man was introduced the crown some were booing and the others were laughing at the western hat.

The cowboy never had a friend in the theater.
They were making fun of how he looked.

6045 Tommy starred at the red ignoring the crowed of New York City slickers they could not insult tommy no matter what they said tommy now was in the manipulation mood.

That angered tommy made him more determined to get that greaser.
Then in walked Stanley sting
6050 The crowd loved sting.
The whole place cheered at sting appearance.
He was there champ.
And sting was about to destroy this invader cowboy con man

THE THREE ANOUNSERS STARTED TALKING

6055 1 first- said what is this hay seen even doing here he is out classed.
2nd-The second commentator agreed
But said the cowboy must be better then he looks or someone would never have arranged to this match.

3rd -Then the last commentator said, "hold up gentleman"
6060 I was the champ too for Meany years.
. And I was deadly afraid to play a street hustler because they don't even know them self how good they are the only time they shoot is just a little better then there Aponte (Now believe me) the cowboy is one of the best street
6065 hustlers in the game! And here is the bad news the cowboy con man will bring that street hustle to this game try a bate Mr. Sting into trying long shots every trick in the book street hustlers are very tricky.
I am predicting the cowboy con man will find a way to win or
6070 make thing very interesting or hard for Mr. Sting.

Then the main announcer took over.

The cameras showed around the gold fingers theater it was a packed theater at Gold fingers.

075 TOM SIENOR AND JOSEPGH was sitting in the front row.

Joseph said to tom I have a felling deep down that tommy won't quiet.

I think tommy can win and he is eighty to one. I am going to bet a little on the cowboy con man,

Tom answered Joseph I have the same feeling.

80 TOM SIENOR PULLED OUT TWO THOUSAND CASH AND TOLD JOSEPH TO BET IT ON TOMMY. JOSEPH SMILLED AND DID THE SAME.

PISTED OFF -Stanley sting ready to destroy that insulting cowboy con man (prick) Send that hillbilly back to wear he came from.

6085

Very serious Cowboy Con Man

6090   The referee was setting up the first rack the game was close.

It was time for the coin toss.
The referee through the coin high in the air the cowboy calls tails.

6095   Tails it was the cowboy won the break.

Everyone thought the cowboy was going to blow the balls all over the table like a bar hustler would do.
But the cowboy shoots smoothly ticked off the middle red opened two balls to the left
6100   but with perfect wait the queue ball slowly bounced off the top rail and slowly rested behind the green.
Sting had nothing he was shocked and couldn't even hit a rail to hit a red

Sting walked around the table and could not figure a shoot;
6105

He tried putting spin on but missed and hit the blue ball costing him five points.
Plus, giving the cowboy two open reds.

The cowboy shot slowly the red dropped then the black.

10 The cowboy shot harder and got and broke out four red.
Then it was cowboy time the cowboy had to take a chance and cut the red in and try
and break all the red out of the glued together rack
. Cowboy amid and pulled the trigger
The red went straight in the corner and the reds spread all over the table.
15

The cowboy ran the table and Drew first blood.
Sting looked surprised and irritated
The cowboy watched sting then sting looked at the cowboy tommy blow sting a kiss.

20 The announcers were speechless and the crowed was a lot quite now.

    1- FIRST GAME WINNER THE COWBOY CON MAN

    2-Second game the con man broke the ball but this time shot at the corner then
25   bounced off the bottom rail with perfect wait leaving the queue ball frozen on the
    red balls of the rake.

    Mr. Sting had to shot on a frozen red.

30   Sting shoot two cushions and left the queue ball at the far end of the table the con
    man hit the rack in the middle then the queue ball with perfect wait the ball
    stopped on the top rail behind the yellow.
    Sting was hocked again.
    Sting looked at the con man with a nasty glare.
35   The con man showed sting a finger and said you like little boys.
    And then gave the cowboy shit smart shit eating grin.

    2- Mr. Sting went crazy; fuck you sting yelled."
    3-
40   4- Then the referees sending both sting and the con man to their dressing rooms.

    5- The referee told both to cool down this is getting away out of line we are in
      public
    6- In ten minutes, we were called back.

6145

7- "Sting was so fucking mad you could see it was all over his face"

8- He was insulted and wanted out of there.

9- Sting tried a terrible hard shot and left the con man open the con man ran thirty-four points to stings zero.

6150

10-Then taking no chances, the con man glued the queue ball right against the rail Behind the green

Sting was hocked again.

STING WAS GETTING FUSTRATED, sting wanted to shoot but never got a chance too.

6155

Sting tried to leave the con man tough but missed leaving the con man an open red.

That was it the con man run most of the table before missing.

But there wasn't enough left on the table sting could not win frustrated sting conceded the second game

6160

10- TWO WINNES COWBOY CON MAN Stanley sting zero

Game three--

The cowboy broke the third game, same thing leaving the queue on the far top rail with precise wait Hocking sting on his first shot.

6165

Sting was starting to sweat and his eyes were glaring with anger.

Sting missed again the con man racked up 24 points and then stuck the queue behind the black.

6170

Sting was hocked again;

Somehow sting hit two rails and cut a red into the side pocket it was a nice shot.

Sting was right on this time.

6175

Every shot was strait in as if he was a machine.

Winning the third game

Sting was starting to shoot;

Mr. Sting ran the whole table ran over a century Mr. Sting won the third game with tremendous shooting

6180

Stanley sting was showing his class.

The crowd was saying sting is back,

85   THAT fucking cowboy is in trouble now?
STING WON third GAME.

Game four

Sting broke the balls and left the cowboy hocked on the top rail.
90

The con man tried to hit a red but miss hit another red but got lucky and hocked sting in the middle of the table the queue ball was frozen on the black

The cowboy shot was just lucky the spectators were yelling
95   Sting looked at the cowboy then said fucking lucky bastard the all the cowboy did was grin. Fuck the cowboy bothered sting just the look of him.

MR Sting missed his shot and left a strait in red the cowboy played some English and got shape on the black perfectly this was all or nothing.
00

The cowboy took the chance and cut the black in the corner than smashed the rack of red balls hoping he would he would get shape on another red.
 Try some cowboy luck.
Sure, enough there were four reds open
05   the cowboy ran four blacks and then with perfect wait went two rails and parked the queue ball behind the brown ball perfect sting was shocked.

Sting was about to flip saying your lucky mother fucker then shaking his head in disbelieve sting now was sweating he was careering a towel.
10

Sting was hocked again.
 Sting was starting to lose it. Sting shot and missed.
 And carelessly left the cowboy open
That was all the cowboy needed and ran the rest of the ball off.

The referee called a brake.
15

Gold Fingers New York

6220 ## "And gave and order you two settle down"

"Cowboy con man three wins- Stanley sting one win"

The announcer was speaking
The cowboy con man has been coning Mr. Sting

6225   The con man is bating sting into trying hard long shots.
And getting away with it

Sting is much the best, his spin and the way Mr sting shoots he's smooth, the cowboy shoots like street hustler.

230   But the con man is manipulating the game and is in control.
"Third announcer"
I TOLD YOU ABOUT A STREET HUSTELER THERE EXPERTS at manipulating putting to sleep their opponents and the aggravating part of the hustle, Mr. sting is not used to this......... THE COWBOY IS DOING IT TO STANLEY STING.

235

THE SECONT ANOUCER SAID WELL THE COWBOY ONLY HAS TO WIN ONE OF THE NEXT THREE TO WIN.
THE PRESSURE IS CLEARLY ON STING NOW.

240   BACK IN THE DRESSING ROOM STING WAS THROWING THINGS ALL OVER THE ROOM UPSET WANTED TO KILL THAT DIRTY BASSTARD COWBOY CON MAN) calling me a homo in public I'll fuck him up now.

Tommy was holding the spirits that came alive inside him and stroking the diamond
245   Brady around the sparking purple sapphires. Very confidante

The referee opened the door lets finish this contest and looked straight at tommy and smiled.

250   # Game five- cowboy three wins – Mr. Sting one wins

The crowd was restless as MR sting was facing elimination plus the millions of New York dollars bet on their champion.
The cowboy broke the balls
255   Leaving sting nothing to shot again Sting had to use two cushions just to hit a red.
Sting was on the top rail frozen against the rail behind the green

Strait behind the green sting went two rails and hit the red braking one red out.

260   The cowboy shot hard and bounced off the rail and flocked a red and broke out the

Whole rack

Then shot a black and another black the cowboy ran six black balls.

6265 And was set up for more
Then Sting yelled THIS HILLBILLY COCKSUCKER is about to take me down.

THE COWBOY PROCEEDED TO POT IN A PINK

6270 THEN STING THROUGH HIS QUE CROSS THE TABLE AND YELLED YOU'RE THE LUCKYEST COCKSUCKER I EVER SEEN.

THEN IT WAS LIKE A SNOW STORM OF LOSEING BET TICKETTS THOUGH OVER THE GLASS (IT WAS OVER)
6275

THE COWBOY CON MAN DEFEATED STANLEY STING.

THE NEW YORK ANOUNCER'S
First talked to Stanley sting (AGAIN)
6280 The announcer said the cowboy was very lucky tonight yes sting said it's hard to beat lady luck
The cowboy was so lucky the queue ball none of those leaves were planed he was lucky

He never had control on the queue ball it just rolled into safety by accident.
6285 Even the cowboy was surprised." (Yes, the announcer agreed)

Then Mr. Sting said the cowboy con man won't be around long he will be a flash in the pan.
And that attitude plus that shit eating grin the cowboy upset me accusing me of liking
6290 little boys and many more terrible things. Plus blowing kisses that Brassard.

But that is the cowboy's only weapon and the actions of a common street hustler moves.
The finger and throwing kisses at Mr. Sting was classless.
6295 That shook sting up he was aggravated and insulting.
The crowd started booing and then all the white tickets were crumpled and throw over the glass; it looked like a hail storm.
They were mad and yelling at the refereed why did you let that ignorant cowboy con man talk like that to Mr. Sting.

300   The announcer then agreed with sting this was the worst match I ever seen he added
       (Sting shouted this cowboy is a cheating bustard.)
       His insulting mouths never chute up.
       Then sting asked the referee why didn't you disqualify that cheating brassard.

305   The referee just walked out saying it's not legal to talk.

       Then the announcer looking mad then called the con man over.

       First question was how's it feels to win your first match against a class player.

310   you cheated cowboy your talking upset sting and you took advantage of that.

       The con man replied well lady luck is hard to beat,
       and nobody told me I couldn't talk!

15   Then the announcer waved the camera away ending the interview.
       The camera went away from the interview and that was the end.

       It was obvious the announcer was clearly on the champion Stanley stings side.

20   One thing they didn't know was the cowboy just pulled off the biggest gamble ever in
       the snooker world.
       That won't get out until the cowboy collects the two million.
       The cowboy con man coned everyone maybe (by accident)

25   Then Joseph yelled and grabbed Tommy and said let's get out of here.

       Joseph then said tom senior wants to talk to you right now let's go.

30   Tommy and Joseph went to the dressing room and collected tommy things.

       Then out the side door fire exit to josephs limo
       We drove straight to the Donnelly mansion in old Manhattan.
       We walked into the study and both tom senior and tom Jr. we're looking at tommy and
35   waiting to hear what tommy had to say.

They both had serious looks and burning mafia eyes.
 Tom senior opened the meeting.
With a sorely question he ask tommy when did you know you could beat sting.

6340

(THIS WAS A SERIOUS MEETING)
Because if they thought tommy coned them it would be bad. Maybe overshoe time

Tommy answered well sir I had the feeling I could beat sting right from the start I told
6345   you that all you guys would say was Look at the people he has beating he has defeated
almost every hot stick in the whole country.
Tommy, you haven't beat anyone.
You had no confidence in me.
But I was going to try I could not tell you to bet on me when I thought I might get beat.
6350   Plus, you guys never had any confidence in me.
Then Joseph said we could have made millions on this tonight.
Then tom senior asked how much did you made tommy.

 Tommy guessed Well I think around two and a half million.
6355   (Holy fuck Joseph said)
Tommy then said if I lost my money.
 I am a gambler that's what I do.
But if I told you guys to bet on me and I lost that's losing your money.

6360   Plus, I never hide anything because tom I gave you ten thousand to bet for me too.

Then (TOM SIENOR SAID)

We were working our per cent age we received from the off-track betting we should
have bet lots it's our fault. Tommy you're the fucking bravest man I ever seen you had
6365   no friends no backers you eat everyone bullshit and worked you owe con.
Tom senior walked over to tommy and hugged tommy then saying you're the best I
ever seen and I am proud we are family.

 Because that's right tommy you gave me ten thousand and I bet it for you Tommy
6370   Tommy never tried to con us!
We WERE TO STUPIED NOT TO BET.

Joseph said but Sting looked to good.
Than tom senior asked even now if that match was on tomorrow would you bet
375 tommy?

Everyone said a little bit.
Stanley Sting is still the champion (then tommy started smiling) and said bull the
cowboy had him from the start?
380

And tommy said I had to play a hell of a safety game to win anyway.
Plus, Sting got so frustrated with the finger and blowing kisses at him all night.

I wonder if he does go both ways.
85 That's what got to Mr. Sting.

Joseph laughs and said that fucked sting up tommy how or what made you attack sting.
Tommy answered well I had to do something I didn't want to be a sacrificial lamp for
sting.
90 TOM SIENOR AND JOSEPH STARTED TO LAUGH.

Then tom senior said well we sure missed a big money day.
Plus, it was mostly Italian.
But tommy is right he never ever told us not to bet on him.
95 Even I placed ten thousand for tommy at 60 TO 1 AND I STILL THOUGHT THE CON MAN
WAS CRAZY TO BET THAT.

Then tom senior said we knew about the other ten thousand you sprinkled around
brown town Delaware.
00 That was a smart move tommy.
Well it was our mistake;
We have to congratulate tommy he pulled it off on his own with no support from us.

(The Cowboy Con Man conned the entire state of New York and pulled it off)
05 Then tom rang the bell for herald to bring some Drinks.

Everyone was astonished by the con that tommy pulled off right in front of their eyes.

"Still there was a little of you must have known more"

6410   Tommy, they said that the rest of the night.
Tommy ducked there questions all night smiling.

Then tommy said please I have had enough of this big city.
I need to move on some ware.
6415

Tom senior said let us know when you're leaving tommy and tipped his glass.
Yes, sir tommy answered as tommy slipped out to the guest house. There felt like there
was at least 5000 pounds lifted off Tommy's back as he walked to the guest house.

6420   Tommy woke up with a head pounding hang over.
Time to clear my head and look at more of dad's letter of places to go.

The letter dad gave tommy pointed directly at brown town Delaware.

6425   Tommy was going to collect the rest of the bet.
Well that ten-thousand-dollar bet on the cowboy con man will ruin things in Delaware
for any kind of set up for the cowboy con man tommy was finished snooker was over.

Tommy had coffee with Joseph the next morning Joseph told tommy don't even try to
6430   hustle again you might get killed we can't protect you there's to many enemies
Tommy answered yes, it's finished I think.

Tommy asked Joseph can you find me a good deal on a motor home (nice one) class
6435

Joseph said I'll look around
Tommy smiled. Joseph said you're on your way aren't you.

Yes, tommy answered as fast as I can the open road is calling.
6440   Joseph said I knew it.
Good luck down that road and whatever the Cowboy Con Man gets into?

Tommy then said I can put my belongings in the motor home and sleep there to.

6445   Tommy said I need a welder to weld a good safe onto that motor home.

Tommy asks Joseph please try and fine me a nice one tommy wants class.
 And out of here quickly.
With one of your discounts you know.
50   Joseph (smiled ok)

For the next three days' tommy stayed at the guest house planning the next best place
to go too.
Tommy called mom and dad
55   Dad already know about the win and was excited first question how much did you win
Tommy answered around one and a half million.

 Dad said well-done tommy. I know you can beat anyone if you put your mind to it.
 Send that back here I'll set your portfolio up for life.
60   I'll buy more grass land and more cattle. Tommy said please build me a nice new house.
Dad said that's one thing I will be sure to do.

Tommy said I'll send it to the royal bank account.
 Then I have to keep four hundred thousand for seed money.
65   Ok dad said.
Then Dad asked you are all along in the biggest city in the world you took everyone on
by yourself.
Here's your mother.
Viola was talking so fast tommy could not understand her and then mom caught
70   herself. She started telling tommy you watch that big city woman.
 They will con you tommy!
Yes, mom tommy said they can't con me mom.

You just be care full, yes mom then mom said you get home in not more than two
75   weeks.
Tommy said I'll try mom.
Then mom said hers your father.
Dads said finish the hustlers list
 And then come home
80

 Dad told tommy maybe after the New York Stanley sting thing you better stop for a
while.
And you better stay away from Baltimore they will know all about New York.

They will be waiting for you;
6485 You can't take the edge there right now.
    Take your father's advice stop shooting snooker for a while.
    Tommy said yes dad I think your right.
    Tommy told Dad tell mom I will be a little bit longer.

6490 Yes, tommy "dad said get out of the east coast.

    Try something ells go back training horse's.
    OK TOMMY said I don't feel like doing anything right now.

6495 We'll let the smoke clear.
    Dads said again get out of the east coast.

    Ok bi for now.
    Then Dad reminded tommy you sent most of that money home.
6500 Yes, tommy said I still have to collect the brown town cash than I'll send it to the Royal
    Bank in High River "FROM DELAWARE" OK Dad said.

    The next day Joseph came over the see tommy at the guest house.
    Tommy was packing all his belongings' Joseph said you're getting ready to travel."
6505
    Yes, tommy answered.

    Joseph asks do you still want a nice motor home
    Tommy answered yes Joseph what have you found.
6510
    Joseph told tommy a friend of the family has A 32-foot regency it very nice has
    everything and it's only one-year-old.

    Tommy said how much." Joseph said half of what it's worth.
6515
    ' TOMMY 'AND WHATS THAT.
    Joseph said I got him down to $22.000.00.
    It's a class ride Joseph said.
    Plus, it supposed to be worth $ 50.000.00.
6520

Let's go right now tommy said.

Joseph said bring the cash. "Yes, I get it tommy answered.

25   Out the door and into josephs limo on the way to the other mafia family's place

Joseph told tommy don't try and jaw him.
Then winked: Tommy nodded.
When we got there the boss of their family showed us and we walked inside the palace
30   with wheels on.

It was so new there still was plastic on the sets.
Nice pink and gray interior.

35   With stained glass cut with lady fingers even a safe under the one cabin
It had a Gm motor train it was Regence.
The best of the best

Joseph introduced tommy to his Irish brother;
40

He congratulated the cowboy on defeating Stanley sting.
Tommy said thanks sir. He didn't care about talking the old Irishman said son you got
the twenty-two thousand cash.
Tommy pulled out the twenty thousand cash.
45   And told the Irish gentleman that's all I have sir.
Ok you own it cowboy. The man said.

Then Joseph asks can you arrange license plates and insurance for tommy for a year.

50   The man smiled I'll pay for that. I'll help to get the Cowboy on the road.
Thanks Joseph said. When can you have it ready to travel?

Give me two days. It's a done deal. Pay him tommy.
The man said the cowboy is hitting the road.
55

I feel sorry for the poor snuck tommy runs into this old country boy.

Then everyone laughs
 We all shook hands and. Joseph told his friend deliver it to Manhattan you know our
6560   address.
 Yep two days!

We left.
Then Joseph had to collect more protection money.
6565   So, tommy rode in the limo all fucking day.

The motor home arrived it was even nicer it was clean all the plastic was gone it was
plash.
Tommy immediately started moving in.
6570   Then Tommy slept in his new home at the Manhattan family estate.
 Tommy went over the night before and told everyone he was heading out early in the
morning.
 And thanked them all.
Tom senior and all told tommy if there anything he needs we are here for you.
6575

 Then Joseph gave tommy the directions to contact his private phone tommy call me
direct. No more polo billiards.
 .

6580

6585

CHAPTER 25
"THE DELAWARE affair and the double con"

Tommy woke up at 4:30 in the morning, started up the palace with wheels and the front gate security opened the gate and tommy waver bi the guard smiled and waved yelled good luck con man.

And out onto the empty Manhattan streets.

To high way 95 south before the morning traffic started

The sun was coming up as tommy went up the ramp onto south 95 Ramp 16a.

The high way mile's sign reed ninety-five miles to Wilmington DELAWARE

BROWN TOWN WAS A PART OF WILLMINGTON.

First hwy 95 went through New Jersey and then Pennsylvania.

Tommy entered the turn pike into Pennsylvania **within a few** minutes he was taking **the** bridge **over the mighty Delaware River to the first state in the union Delaware**

It was a feeling of relief from the big New York City
And the pressures of the hustlers every ware
Tommy could see a man getting eaten up there very easily and tommy was looking forward to what lays ahead in Delaware.
Tommy now was free with an open mind happy looking for fun and he had heard this was the State that started the ladies of the "Southern Bell", incent beautiful woman?

It was just a few minutes to the sign
Right turn for Wilmington off from Interstate 95

The big regency was nice and it felt free.

6620   No more limos, no more questions.
Tommy pulled onto the old streets of Brown Town he parked the regency.
Continued to walk to the first bookie joint where he bet FIVE THOUSAND BUCKS at 60 TO 1 ODDS.
Tommy showed the winning ticket to the window teller he seemed shocked.
6625

The bald man then said, "excuse me sir".

Within five minutes the boss had walked out he then looked at tommy and said, "you pulled a big one-off cowboy".
6630   "We never knew you were the Cowboy Con Man or we would have never taken that bet".
Tommy then replied, "nobody asked me you just grabbed my five thousand cash". Like you found it
Well come into my office.
6635   Tommy followed the man to a back office the man offered tommy a drink.

Tommy said have you got a cup of coffee yes set down cowboy.

Then the bald man said I am not paying you until you make an appearance here tonight
6640   and tell everyone that you bet your five thousand at sixty to one.

And enjoy yourself with complementary drinks or dinner
OK TOMMY agreed.
They shook hands and the man said sees you to night around nine cowboys
6645   Yes, tommy said.
Then out the door to the next bookie joint
Tommy walked in and went to the betting windows there was an older fat lady there and looked at Tommy's ticket, her eyes got big and said wait please.
In a few minutes out peaked a man from the office door looked at tommy and was
6650   excitedly talking to someone on his phone.
(Last thing he said was the cowboy in here right now)
Then that got some kind of response.

THE MAN CAME OVER TOMMY GREETED him.
6655   THE COWBOY CON MAN
Well my boss is on his way and then he continued to sit the cowboy down at a table

awaiting the boss.

I five minutes in walked a young Italian man walked straight over and stuck out his
60   hand and said you're the cowboy con man.
It's a real pleasure to meet you cowboy
How did you beat Stanley sting?
Tommy smiled, "Mr. Sting is just too high strung",

65   Mr. Sting could not take country boys insults.

Tommy smiled.
Then he said, "I'll bet you won't try that again cowboy".

70   Tommy agreed then replied, "Mr. Sting is still the champ sir".
He said, "That's what I thought".

Then he paid the cowboy off.
Three hundred thousand big ones
75   Then the Italian boss asked would you play sting again.

The cowboy answered as he was walking out the door.

'Yes" but we will have to wait until Mr. Sting get over his heart break!
80

Then out the door tommy went.
It was only one in the early afternoon.
Tommy waved at a cab and it pulled over and tommy jumped in the cab driver asked
ware to sir.
85   Tommy said take me to the race track Delaware downs.
The cab driver said that's in Stanton. Ok tommy asks it's not far is it. Nope just up the
hill.
Then away they went when they entered the front gate it was beautiful.
Tall trees and green grass
90   The old classy grandstand it was old but well cared for the cab driver was a gambler he
told tommy that Delaware Park was built by the DuPont family Delaware's royal family.
The DuPont family sold all the gun power to any ship or anyone that needed gun
powder.

Including the civil war, and any pirate ship that needed it

6695   They made millions in the early 1800.

DELAWARE PARK

6700

WE drove back to Wilmington back down interstate 95
There at the main entry to Wilmington was a bunch of serves' stations and restaurants.
There was a nice restaurant and bar called Fridays.
Tommy said I'll treat you to lunch the cabbie said at Fridays.

6705   Tommy said yes sir, the cabbie was happy.

Tommy got a lot of info from the cabbie.
Tommy asked the cabbie this Friday's looks like it would be busy at night.

6710   Yes, the cabbie said all the yuppies come here some of the trainers from
Delaware Park
Tommy noticed a nice garden inside water fountains and brass rails.

Class place! And the food was excellent.

The cabbie showed tommy three more bookie joints were.

15   All in underground back doors

The cabbie never asked who tommy was just called tommy country boy as he dropped tommy at the motor home that was parked on the street.

20   Tommy needed to have his afternoon sleep
Dad said it was the secret to long japery plus tommy had to show up at that bookie joint to get his money at nine tonight.
Then tommy is out of Delaware.
Tommy was extra tired woke up at five thirty.
25   Had a shower and put on a white shirt and jeans cowboy hat and riding boots.

Then set the electric steps of the regency to stay down.

Looking for a nice class bar or lounge at the end of brown town there was a nice-
30   looking place called (Fridays)

They are a franchise all over the world in every country they were real popular and nice.
Tommy walked up and looked inside. Man, it was even nicer the Fridays on the
35   interstate in New York.
Looked around and set at the bar and ordered gin soda.

There was a racing form on the bar.
It was from Delaware Park. Tommy asked the waitress if he could look at the racing
40   form.
She said yes help yourself.
Tommy set and sipped the gin and soda and studying the racing form.
It took tommy around forty-five minutes to study the ten-race program at Delaware Park.
45   Tommy heart was horse racing.
It was tommy passion.
It was seven o'clock now.
And the cowboy con man had to show up at the bookies and tell everyone I bet with the bookie and he paid me in cash and he is honest all that.

6750   The crowed of gamblers were very friendly and liked the cowboy con man.
Tommy never took so many pictures in his life sign every picture.
It was nice be away too much exposure for tommy.

6755   (Tommy could see snooker was over ;)
There would be no snooker again. The hustle was over? They all asked the same
question you got to Mr. Sting you manipulated him would you play him again Mr. Sting
will be wise to your game?

6760   (TOMMY WOULD SAY THE SAME THING OVER and over MR STING IS STILL THE CHAMP)
THEY ALL SMILLED AND AGREED. They like the con man answer.
Tommy said good bye and got out of that bookies joint
Not before the owner paid the cowboy off in cash so everyone could see.

6765   Then out the door!
Tommy had all the cash $600.000.00. Stopped at the regency there was a safe welded
into the frame. Under the closet put the balance cash in.
Then walked up the street too Fridays night club.

6770

6775

CHAPTER 26

MEETING THE GIRL OF TOMMYS DREAMS

Tommy walked in and set at the end of the long bar, ordered a Heineken beer in was nice cold it was perfect.

Just behind tommy there was a table of people,

They were a group of horse trainers from Delaware part.

Talking about the horses they ran in today's racing program at Delaware PARK.

Tommy listened for a long time.

It was very interesting to tommy;

There were three beautiful ladies and two men.

All were trainers.

Tommy told the bar maid to take them a round of drinks Time to make a move?

After their drinks were delivered the bar maid pointed to tommy that's ware this round of drinks came from.

They looked at the cowboy at the bar and all said thanks cowboy.

The one lady said is that a real cowboy or a city cowboy.

And smiled

Then tommy said I am just traveling though originally from a cattle ranch way up in Alberta Canada.

I am lost tommy said but very interested in horse racing.

Then they asked do you know anything about race horses.

Tommy answered well I trained horse's all my life little here and there.

From cow horses to race horse's that's why I wanted to talk to you.

Yes, tommy said I am a small trainer not as advanced as you people.

The girl that intrigued tommy started asking question how did you got here Tommy and smiled.

Tommy answered I drove down just got through visiting family in New York.

And then tommy asks the lady her name.

She answered my name is Lisa.

Then tommy and Lisa shook hands slowly something happened when our hands touched.

6815   Lisa then said I live on the back side of Delaware Park and I have a large stable.

Then tommy was introduced to the rest all very nice.

Tommy then asked to have you got a runner or two.

Lisa said no just claimers.

Tommy then asked Lisa how many horses are you are training.

6820   She smiled only ten head.

We had several more drinks.

The other trainers all left said morning comes quickly.

Lisa told tommy I have a couple horses that can run just haven't got it out of them yet.

6825   (That got tommy gabling ear)

But it was hard to think about business at this time.

Tommy couldn't help to notice the beautiful curves of Lisa body and the way she moved she was wearing a pink wool sweater with a gold Diamond horse shoe necklace and it looked expensive.

6830   When it came to her breasts they had to be at least size 38 D. and stuck strait out.

And a natural blonde no artificial it was real.

Beautiful light brown eyes

6835   White complexion not a small girl around one hundred and thirty pounds

We were all alone and we both became silent.

We both know where was magical things we are going on between us.

6840   Tommy slowly put his hand on Lisa's leg and massaged ever so smoothly up and down each time moving closer to her inner thighs.

She didn't stop tommy now Lisa's breathing got almost out of control then Lisa leaned towards tommy and quickly whispered in Tommy's ear

6845

I have got to get out of heir or I'll end up doing something on a first date that a class girl like me just don't do...

But rest assured cowboy tommy Lisa said I definitely want to see you again how about tomorrow if that's alright of course.

6850   Then Lisa told tommy where she lived and where to park the regency and Lisa's phone number.

We kissed and tommy felt her breasts.
Then tried to steady her breath
We were in full agreement we planned to meet tomorrow
55 Around eleven after the morning training was finished.

Tommy walked back to the regency and went straight to bed.
Parked on the brown town street

60 The morning garbage truck woke tommy up.
It was five thirty,
Tommy showered and shaved and dressed.

Put his nicest white shirt on.
65 Started up the regency and drove to the truck stop to have coffee.

It took tommy a long time to wake up suffering from a hangover.

In an hour tommy was feeling good woke up.
70

And then drove to the back gate where Lisa stable would be.

Then parked the regency and walked to the security at the stable gate.

75 Then paged Lisa, the announcement from the speakers was trainer Lisa pretty man
visitor ay the west gate.
Tommy waited nervously; in a few minutes, there she was smiling signed tommy in and
off to her stable Lisa was in the middle of working two of her horses.
Head to head they worked.
80 Went fast the first 3/8 mile then flattened out in the finish.
It was clear to tommy neither horse was ready to run. But Lisa thought they did well?

After Lisa was finished the morning training we went for lunch.
Lisa then said I didn't know if I would ever see you again country boy from Alberta
85 Canada.
Then tommy using the con man ways, said the most suiting thing he could think of.

6890 Tommy never sleep all night thinking of that beautiful horse trainer and now my dream came true can I buy you a nice lunch (yes Lisa said)

After lunch Lisa showed all her horses in her stable.
Tommy never said anything; But Lisa had a lot to learn she was a spoilt rich girl.

6895 Then Lisa asked, Tommy can you help me in the morning by walking the hot horse's in the morning I will pay you $4 dollar each.

Tommy said what time do I start boss.
Lisa smiled and said you be there at six o'clock.
6900

Then Lisa took tommy to the racing office to get her new hot walker a hot walker's license.
Lisa filed the form out.
Tommy signs the form.
6905 In ten minutes, the license man came back and told Lisa.
Mr. Thomas marks Donily is no hot walker Lisa.
Lisa said well just who is this man?
THE LICENSEING clerk told Lisa he is one of the most dangerous horse Trainers in America. He was leading long shot trainer in sports Illustrated
6910 .
Won the long shot illustrated Magazine, this man brought in more long shots then any trainer in North America two years ago.

Plus Mr. Tommy Marks Doily have an alias (HE IS THE COWBOY CON MAN) just cleaned
6915 out New York City with a brilliant setup.

LISA that man is famous he Just defeated the New York snooker champion Mr. Stanley sting in a big match it was simulcast all over even to Delaware park
They call him the best street hustler now he beats the best Stanley sting.
6920

Quotation on his name is that he is the best at what he does', Gentleman slow talking country boy, but deadly.

The cowboy has lots of talent snooker (the other horse racing).
6925

Lisa what is going on this man is no hot walker.
He is the Cowboy con man for real!

Lisa stopped and looked at "this man is no hot walker."
30   LISA looked at tommy and did not believe one thing that the clerk told her.

Then slowly told the clerks go ahead license him he is working for me.

He shook his head and completed the hot walker license.
35

Then handed the card to Lisa and said look out Lisa you got yourself the real cowboy
con man in living flesh.

ON the way, back to Lisa's barn
40   Lisa was silent not knowing what to say.

SHE finally said can you tell me the truth now cowboy and promise to be honest with
me tommy Lisa wondered if she could trust tommy.
Then tommy said I am always honest Lisa.
45   Everyone sets there self-up.

And I just finished a big con in New York was gambling big time with the Italians
against Mr. Stanley sting? I am finished for a long time.
Even I thought the champion of New York was better than me.
50

Tommy explained I shook him up by talking to him;
Mr. Sting didn't like what I was saying so it through his professional snookers game off
a little.
Lisa asked what you said to him that made him so mad
55   Tommy said things like
That he dressed like a homeo.
And later, he liked little boys and are you a cross dresser.
Lisa asks how much did you make.

60   Well that's what I was doing when we met in brown town.
The Two bookies owed me six hundred thousand.
And they paid me yesterday.

Lisa said how much did you make totally!

6965   Tommy answered around two million.
Lisa looked stunted.

So, where and what's your next sting?
Tommy told Lisa well I was going to go to Baltimore there a couple pool hustlers at a
6970   place called the California inn.
But I think I better let the cowboy cool off for a while.
Lisa said that bar or night club is just outside laurel race track.
There's a famous man there called Larry Lamparter he owns that place he has horses.
Tommy asked can I hang around with you for a while.
6975   Lisa looked and finally said yes but promises no con here.
No tommy said I wouldn't do that,
Tommy then said I am almost in love with you Lisa.
We are a match,
Didn't you feel the electric energy when we held hands last night?
6980
Oh, tommy Lisa said yes, I did and it felt right
Tommy then said if it felt right then it is right.
Then we held hands on the way back to her barn it was the same feeling again we
were a match.
6985   Tommy said Lisa let me show you my hotel on wheels.
It's better than the Hilton
Lisa said it's out in the parking lot isn't it
Tommy said it has its own water and electric supply.

6990   Lisa said let's go look at where the cowboy con man lives.
We took Lisa's truck out to the parking lot and parked beside the 32-foot Regency.

When we stepped up the stairs automatically came down and into the motor home
Lisa looked and said this is real nice strait class cowboy.
6995
Lisa still thought tommy was an innocent country boy witch tommy was.

Tommy said I have a cold beer in the frig Lisa said yes lets.

000   Tommy and Lisa then drank the beer and tommy started to do what came naturally.

Tommy dropped one big breast out and gently polled it down.
Then started sucking her big nipple
Then in around 5 minutes the other breast Lisa was breathing hard.
005

Then tommy wasted no time and down her panties then off they went

Then Lisa pulled off Tommy's shirt then his pants tommy spread Lisa's legs and in a rush
10   Mounted her quickly

It was rough and fast.
Then tommy blow his load the sperm shot up inside Lisa she felt the hot sperm there was at least eight shots of sperm and LISA started screaming and giving tommy all her
15   excepting all.
They lay there for at least an hour and then tommy started again.

They made love at least eight times.

20   They were both existed but the cowboy fell very much in love with Lisa pretty man.

Tommy thought partners they just had to be. Lisa had hackles on both sides plus on her neck and both breasts.
Lisa agreed
25   And then Lisa asked tommy how you get those horses to run so fast
Just at that persist time win and win all the money.
You're a gambler.
Then get that great handle of leading long shot trainer of the year.
In sports Illustrated Magazine, (Leading long shot trainer of the year)
30   Lisa asked to tell me what you gave those horses cowboy.

Tommy set back and looked innocent.
But now tommy was tip off.
Lisa wasn't in love,
35   She just wanted the mother load to enhance a race horse's performance.

Tommy said dear it's all in the training,
Tommy can read a horse's mind I know what they're thinking.

7040   Then got up and started to clean up around the regency and ignored Lisa's questions.

But now the cowboy had a feeling of entrust this lady wants information.

Lisa knew something was not right between the cowboy and her.
7045

Lisa didn't know what to do or say.
She said I'll call you and felt.
Tommy never said anything just let Lisa go.

7050   The next morning

Lisa called and said tommy could you come and ride the saddle horse for me.

I had a problem with the regular rider he is drunk every day.

7055   And I have two horses that have to go to the starting gate this morning.
Tommy took a few seconds before answering Lisa said (please) then tommy said I'll be
there in ten minutes.
Lisa was happy and said we are waiting.
Tommy walk into the shadow Lisa was saddling a horse.
7060

Tommy seen the saddle horse tied in front of the racing barn.

Then never used the stirrup just swung on.

7065   Then Lisa lead the horses and exercise rider to the end of the shed row and told tommy
watch out this horse can get bad behind the starting gate.

Tommy seen the horses was getting hot just walking to the track.

7070   Tommy's experience told him this horse is going to through a big wreck tommy stop.

Stepped off the saddle horse and put the lead chain under the horse's lip

It's called a lip chain.
075 That would stop the horse's bull shit.
Lisa and her owner were watching from the chokers stand.

The horse was usually a bad starting gate Horses.

80 But this time went straight in tommy on locked the lip chain.
And he was ready to work five furlongs.
Without throwing a wreck if he can get away with it.

The exercise rider told Lisa where you got this pony boy from.
85

Man, he knows what he is doing
That race horse smelled the presents of something and stopped fighting him.
The second horse was the same

90 Just a stern urging not beating the horse
The horse was ok from only one of tommy lesions. He was now paying attention to the
race track.
The owner of the horse told Lisa you finally got some good help.

95 Then Lisa said yes, I am hiring the best people and paying more for them.
Her owner answered I'll help I like it Thanks she said!

Tommy noticed every horse Lisa trained was short;

00 They all flattened out at the end of their work out.

Lisa tracked eight horses that morning.
Lisa worked horses the sane sprint five furlongs,

05 Tommy thinking Lisa was running a sexual con (on the con man)

I am going to find out what kind of class these horses are.
Without Lisa expecting anything?

7110   (THIS JUST MIGHT BE A place to set up could make piles of money.

Lisa ACSADENLY SET UP the whole stable of ten head if so the cowboy will have a great summer half to treat Lisa right.
Now tommy will start a gentleman relationship it's a double con
7115   Lisa will think she succeeded with her sexual con.
But the cowboy will enjoy the ride.

Plus, set up her horse's Lisa is coning those owners. She does not know a fucking thing about training horses.
7120
I half to make her a deal to make things easier for her to concentrate her million air owners.
Tommy continued helping Lisa for around two weeks some of her race horses looked like they were in a feed lot.
7125   Ready for the Pet meat Purina dog food not ready to run.

All The horses had win records in the last two years winning for $75.000.00 in New York plus wins for $62.000.00 and $50.000.00 nice horse's.

7130   Lisa could talk nice and show her breasts off and hold that million-air owner but could not train a chainman too eat rice.

Lisa was panicking there was a lot of pressure her horses were not wining or even running good.
7135
After the afternoon of great sex, we started talking.
Lisa asked what you are going to do tommy.

Tommy answered I have things to do and I need to go shortly.
7140   Then Lisa said I well pay you to help with the horses.

Tommy said ok I am in love with you.

And want to merry you some days;
7145   I don't need your money.

I'll take over training the horses.

Tommy said I will go pick where you're going to run the horses.
50 Lisa, you stay in the club house with the million air owners concentrate on getting more horse.
I will tell you when they're getting close to being ready to run.
Is that a deal

55 Lisa was excited
Yes, tommy I would love to do the mingling.
You visit your owners I will be your barn foreman.
Lisa asked how much would that cost.

60 Tommy then leaned over and said free.
But tell the exercise riders and your grooms to take orders from me.
I want to merry you Lisa.
You stay out of the training.
You are the promoter and walk around looking good and arrange more owners with
65 horses.
"Lisa looked at tommy you will do this for free.
Yep tommy answered? We have a long-term future.
It's a deal Lisa said I don't like five in to morning anyway.

70 Take over tomorrow tommy.
Tommy said please get me the horses racing forms for the last two years on all your horses past performance then I'll know how to train them.

Ok tommy Lisa said I'll get them printed off tomorrow morning.
75

Tommy said then after this is over will you marry me.

As we slipped back on the bed for another afternoon and Lisa's sexual con
Of hers or now it might be the cowboys turn to enjoy.
80

Tommy started training Lisa's out of shape.
Made into sprinters by her way of training

At first the exercise boys would not listen to tommy they sprinted the horses the same
7185   way as when they worked for Lisa.

Tommy fired all three of exercise riders.
Lisa told them to lessen to tommy or we will get other gallop boys.
Then they ask tommy how would you like each horse trained.
7190   Lisa was bringing the owners to watch their horses work.

Tommy changed the way they worked instead of sprinting all the time tommy galloped
the horses three quarters of a mile.
Then let them run the last quarter or 3/8 of a mile.
7195   They never had much left for the end so the owners were disappointed.
Lisa said well he had a bad day.

Then Lisa came back to the barn and asks tommy what is going on.
Tommy said your horses aren't ready to run a race Lisa.
7200   I have to get some miles into them.
Just wait these horses' need around thirty days.

Ok Lisa said I will tell him.
Forty-five days' later tommy told Lisa to enter all the horses.
7205   They are almost ready.
Lisa entered the first horse at the same price claiming race as they ran for her.
Only one horse got in.
The racing form came out her horse was picked last longest shot in the field.
(THE COWBOY IS BACK)
7210   Tommy called Joseph in New York and asked him if he could bet on a horse for tommy.

Ok give me the name and where it is running.
Friday sixth race Delaware Park, $5000.00 to win $2000.00 to place and $3000.00 to
show.
7215   Joseph said done cousin.
Send me the cash to you know where.

Thanks Joseph, it will be there this afternoon special delivery.
Two days tell the race.
7220   Tommy gave the horse a booster shot of a vitamin mixture.

He will get more the day of the race.

Plus, a good pain killer.
Tommy told Lisa to take the horse from off the pace no more sprinters.

25

Set away back let those horses run on the front end.

You horse will run them down the final home stretch ok tommy Lisa said I will give those orders.

30   The race was about to start; the odds were 99 to 1

There off it was a fast track the horses on the front end were going fast first quarter in 22seconds flat.
Half a mile pole 46 flat,

35   That was to fast a pace to continue.

The front runners were fading.
Lisa horse was starting to move.
Down the lane they came on the outside Lisa's horse won easy.

40

Tommy quickly looked at the odds board it was 70 to 1 tommy just made over $135.000.00-
Lisa was excited, grabbed tommy and said let's go to the winner's circle get our picture taken.

45   Tommy declined and said I don't like pictures go yourself.

Tommy walked back to the barn.
And waited for the horse to return from the test barn

50   Looked the horse over the horse was in nice shape.

Tommy told the groom to do him up on all four legs and gave the groom fifty dollars.

Then tommy grabbed a cab and went back to the regency.

55

Lisa never won a race for so long she would be partying.
That's fine with tommy.

Let her talk!
Tommy showered and opened the door over the drivers set and reached up and pulled
7260   out the magical DIAMOND BRADY.

Then out the door to a pool hall not far from where the regency was parked

Tommy was away from the Lisa bullshit and at home with the snooker table and trying
7265   to shoot straight
Tommy was trying the long shots tommy try and put juice on the ball besides making
the shot.
Tommy shot snooker for three hours and was not shooting well.

7270   Tommy forgot doctor Pearls glasses at the regency.

Next time I will shoot I will remember them they really help.

It was a beautiful night in Willington Delaware;
7275
The moon was shining high in the sky tommy walked all the way up the hill from
Wilmington to the city of Stanton that is where the regency was parked and Delaware
Park was located.
Then went to bed it was a good day.
7280
Then at two thirty in came drunk Lisa celebrating her big win.
Tommy never answered her.
Then she slipped off her dress and lay beside tommy.

7285   The she snuggled close and reached into tommy shorts and tommy was hard Lisa
stroked tommy for a few minutes then tommy mounted her quickly.
Lisa knows what turned tommy on.
They never got much sleep;
They made love all night long,
7290   Lisa only wins in two years.
Lisa enjoyed playing the big trainer mingling with the rich people

Tommy was bearded down back at the barn
Tommy knew he wasn't going to be here very long.

295   Just until these three horses ran.
Then tommy was gone.
This con was almost over.
Lisa had three horses in on Saturday.

300   All three horses needed help.
Or they weren't going to get nothing

Tommy went after all three crippled horses.

05   Tommy gave then vitamin shoots then the day of the race

Gave all three injections in the nervous system, the spinal cord all though the tail it
would hold for 36 hours, these would be different horses for the next three days,
 They will become monsters act like they were three-year old's.
10

The endorphins were ten thousand times stronger than morphine with the feeling of a
prize fighter in the best shape the prime of their lives.
 Athlete endorphins were the mother Lode.

15   They can't test for it and it gives the horse a chance to run faster than they ever did in
their life.
 These horses are going to run fast as they ever had in their life.

 Everyone was picked at the bottom of the page
20

Tommy called Joseph tommy asked can you bet again.

 Joseph said depends how much that last one hurt the bookie.

25   Tommy asked isn't there another bookie.

 Ok send the cash how much on what horses. Ok tommy said the note will be with the
cash.
 Ok Joseph.
30   Lisa Pretty man has three old plugs running tomorrow.
There all picked to finish (last) longest shots in their fields.

On each horse bet $5000.00 to win-$2000.00 to place and the show $3000.00.

The same on all three of trainer Lisa prettymans horse bet all three the same.

7335

I'll send you thirty thousand tonight it should be there early tomorrow morning.

Joseph said do you know something or are you gambling
Tommy said Joseph I am going after all three with the cowboy's best drugs.

7340

Ok Joseph said it will be placed somewhere.
Thanks tommy said.
Joseph ask tommy when you are going on the hustle again with that famous Diamond Brady stick.

7345   Tommy answered shortly.

The next morning Lisa never showed at the barn.
She called and said she was sick.
Tommy said too much partying

7350   Lisa never answered.
Tommy only looked after the three horses that were running this afternoon.

Tommy cleaned out all the bedding of all three horses' stalls they were on a drawing up

7355   Even the water was removed.
The horses were getting ready for the run of their lives.
And they know it they pick it up from tommy they had a different look in their eyes.

Their ears were all pined back they had their youth back.
7360   It was nice to see.

IT WAS PADDOCK TIME for the first horse

The third race
7365   As the horse was lead past the odds board. Lisa's first horse was 99-1.

Tommy hoped Joseph got all three bets down.
BIGSHOT Lisa was waiting in the saddling paddock.

Lisa asks tommy what's the orders for the rider to do;

370

Tommy said tell him to sit close 4th or fifth and move when he feels it is the right time.

Lisa left to the club house Lisa had another man with lots of money.

375 Tommy walked into the crowd So Lisa could not find tommy

Then tommy walked down the outside of the track and set in the morning training sets.

Watched the race and it was an exciting one LISA'S horse won easy. Paid 60 to one.

80

The second horse of Lisa's was in the paddock saddling Lisa was drunk but ask Tommy what's the orders this time.
Tommy said setback run the last half a mile.

85 Lisa told the jockey.
Tommy was exited again Lisa was getting drunk.

Tommy went back down to the training sets to watch.

90 Sure, enough Lisa's horse came from off the pace to win.

The announcer said as Lisa was in the winner's circle.

This was trainer Lisa prettymans second win of this afternoon.

95

The third horse was in the saddling paddock.

Lisa was really liquored now.
What's the orders this time tommy.

00

Tommy said setback but move him early in the backstretch.
This old horse won so easy it was called steeling.

After the race Lisa was in the winner's circle three times in one day.
05 Lisa said I won the last four races' straight.

Lisa was celebrating and saying I am going to be the leading trainer!

The cowboy knows everything about spoiled Lisa.

7410   Lisa's father was the development minister for Delaware.

(Then quite that job) and became a Lobbyist in Washington D C.

He was a real politician a real big con man!

7415

Lisa was so spoiled she would do anything to get what she wanted.

And she did not believe what the clerk was telling her.

7420   She looked at tommy and already had him cleaning her stalls for free.

When she heard tommy was no groom (cowboy con man) that made her Qerious and was set out the get what tommy had to offer.

7425   She never figured the cowboy was gambling on her horses and cashed four good gambles.
The cowboy already had the best of her stable those horses were ruthless to tommy!

Lisa was mingling in the club house; all her daddy's friends were congratulating her and
7430   telling Lisa they know she would figure things out and now four straight victories well done Lisa.

Tommy never even went back to the barn.
Caught a cab and went back to the regency

7435

Now tommy was thinking of the California inn just outside of laurel race track Baltimore Maryland.
Tommy was finished with Lisa and all the bull that came with her.

7440   THE NEXT MORNING, tommy was enjoying a nice coffee and steak and eggs at Fridays,
It was nice tommy had a clear mind and on more Lisa and her selfish ways.
Tommy Called Joseph and he answered you mother fucker.

I am taking ten percent.
Tommy answered I would not have it any other way big Joe.

45

Then Joseph asked how in fuck did you enhanced those hoses so fucking much that fast.

Tommy answered again.

50 You're talking to the Cowboy con man
" Joseph. Fuck Joseph said I know? (You have convinced me)!

Tommy was walking back from Fridays to the regency it was around two miles' tommy needed some exercise.

55 When he entered the regency tommy started packing things in drawers and getting ready to hit the famous interstate 95 south to Timonium Maryland then east to laurel. To the famous California inn

Home of Mr. Larry Lamparter the world's hottest diamond Brady

60

This is going to be a real pleasure class man in a class entertainment and snooker hall with one of the finest restaurants in Maryland.

Tommy was ready to hit the Hy way south.

65

Tommy was walking over to the office to pay the regency rent.

In drove Lisa, she was mad and she was dominant.

70 She was asking questions about where were you last night and this morning.

My horses weren't trained this morning.

Tommy answered well you're the trainer aren't you.

75

Yes, I am but you were in charge of that.
No, I was giving you a helping hand
"Lisa then said are you staring back at my barn.
Tommy answered no Lisa I have to go I have big business that was planned for a couple

7480 years now!
"Your leaving Lisa said. "Tommy answered yes I am going not far just to laurel Maryland not far.
Lisa then was ferrous,"
I am pregnant with your kid, "Tommy said I have only been heir for three months how
7485 did that happen so fast. What about the owner of yours you were biz with him?
  Lisa was mad and walked out the regency door.

After Lisa felt
Tommy thought he should stay one more night.
7490

Tommy walked over to a small bar and set and had a beer.

Within thirty minutes the cell phone rang.
 It was Lisa never said hello just told tommy he was invited for supper tomorrow night
7495 my father wants to talk to you;

Ok tommy said what time
Lisa said seven
 Tommy said Ok I'll be there.
7500

Tommy still had some strong feelings for Lisa.
 (But knows she could not be trusted)

But maybe the cowboy could train the strong-willed Delaware girl.
7505

Seven o'clock tommy walk in to the prettymans mention front door Lisa opened the door well just in time.
Lisa introduced tommy to Mr. Prettymans and her mother.

7510 They wasted no time and said come to the dining room for supper.

Everyone had their places at the table, not a word was said will eating.

The air you could cut with your fork.
7515 Then after dinner Mr. Pretty man said we have a few things to talk about
Mr. Con man, come to the living room we have to talk in privet.

"Then Mr. Pretty man said what do you want tommy money as he opened the desk drawer and pulled out a fair amount of cash and said takes this and I never want to see you again (FUCKING CON MAN)

Tommy said no sir shove that where the sun doesn't shine.
"MR pretty then said well you're not getting anything around heir.

Tommy looked at the stupid politician and said I'll bet you I have as much fucking money as you have.
 Mr. Pretty man then said you're not going to con me or any of my family tommy you stay away from my little girl;

I don't need a professional con man close to my family.

Tommy wanted to tell that old ugly bustard just the way tommy felt but held back.

Tommy Simply slipped out the side door and got out of the house without Lisa seeing him.
Tommy walked down the street of New castle Delaware to the first bar and chugged a couple beers down then ordered a whisky.

 It tasted good,
Then in a short time tommy started to figure out Lisa was just like her father.

And if they can't control you they don't want you around that was plain.

It was time to get back to my own biz! Live this bull behind.

            THE DOUBLE SEX CON DIDN'T WORK ON THE COWBOY
I have to tell mamma about this she will be proud.

At day break the regency was headed south on interest 95 Timonium the turned east to laurel Maryland.
Found the California inn and parked in the big parking lot.
Went back to bed and sleep all day tommy was tiered either from pressure or not enough sleep,
After getting out of DELAWARE the sun started shining and the presser was off.

7555 Needs some sleep then start checking out Dads final hustle on the list California inn laurel may land?

Tommy fell to sleep fast.

Woke up at seven thirty that night

Had a coffee just like it was morning showered and thinking this was the way to travel it has everything

7560 Tommy sipped his coffee wondering what he would run into in this fancy gaming theater.

THE CALIFONIA INN FINNAL STOP ON Dad's Hustlers list

Tommy finished his coffee

7565 Then left the Diamond Brady in the Regency

Walked into the California inn

It was a class theater with the best tables and set up like a casino there was a bar tenders all wearing tuxedos.

7570 Tommy tried to find the big hustlers table.

Ordered a gin and seven and walked around then found some guys that looked the part of hustler's smart dressed sharp and talking to go along with their games

7575 Tommy set and watched for a short time sipped the gin it tasted excellent.

Just then there were two big bouncers on both sides of tommy with security on their sleeves.

They both said MR COWBOY don't be alarmed but please look up at the roof there is

7580 an office there behind the stained glass.

And the boss wants to talk to you before you get started hustling in the California inn.

Yes, tommy said I would like to meet Mr. Larry Lamparter.

So, one bouncer leading the way and the other fallowing right behind

7585

We reached the roof office

Then through a door entering Lamparter office

90   Tommy set in front of his desk Mr. Lamparter was ignoring the cowboy for a short
      time.

      Then looked at tommy and said what you are doing in my snooker theater.

95   Tommy said just looking around.
      Mr. Lamparter said you're not going to pull your hustling bull shit in my place Mr.
      Cowboy con man.

      But I'll make you and offer me and you will play.
00
       Ok tommy asked what the odd is
       I mean you have to give me thirty to one right Mr. Lamparter.

      LAMPARTER said look you little bastard.
05   Ten thousand even. Put up ten thousand cowboys and I'll do the same.

       Tommy then said Mr. Lamparter you're the hottest stick in America.
      No way will the cowboy play you even odds.

10   Lamparter said nope if you won't except the challenge please remove yourself from the
      California inn plus that motor home out of here right now.

      Tommy said ok Mr. Lamparter I am out of here

15   Then Larry said not before you eat one of the best Maryland sea food smog's boards
      and it's on me son and one more thing say a big howdy to young Billy your Dad.

       He was the best.
       And stay in your motor home for the night
20   Then shook tommy hand and told tommy he was busy.

      Tommy went and had a free Dinner
       But knowing the cowboy was not welcome here.

25   OR ANYWHERE EILS (THIS HUSTLE WAS OVER)
      TOMMY IS FINNISHED HUSTLING SNOOKER.

The next morning
Tommy headed the regency west to ALBERTA CANADA

7630   GOING HOME FOR A BRAKE AND LET THINGS COOL DOWN.

Need to see mom and Dad AND SPEND SOME WELL NEEDED TIME AT THE RANCH.

LET THE ALBERTA WIND AND SUN AND THE ROLING HILLS OF THE PRAIRY SOAK IN FOR

7635   A WILL.

Crossed the border at sweet grass Montana
Into Alberta and north passed Lethbridge too Lomond when I drove through my home town a thrill came up my spine.

7640

WAVED AT SOME OLD FRIEND AS I DROVE THROUGH TOWN

They waved back and started smiling the cowboy has returned and must have won a big hustle he is driving a quarter mile long house on wheels.

7645

Then west of Lomond five miles and turned north four miles came over the last hill and there it was the marks ranch the 7H RANCH.

Could not wait to enter our drive way stopped the regency and the first one to meet

7650   tommy was my faithful dog tip he was a Irish wolf Hound eight feet tall when standing up.
Old tip knocked tommy to the ground he was so excited.

Then it was Mom and Dad's turn.

7655   Mom started you haven't been eating right and probably drinking too.

Then Dad was saying you did really good tommy really good!

After supper tommy had to get away walk with old tip through the southern Alberta

7660   hills that was our home and we grow up in them.

Tommy was finished hustling snooker; the cat is out of the bag father said.

565 It's now a different game tommy you were right not to take up Mr. Lamparter ten-thousand-dollar challenge; I'LL bet that old bastard still has that eye.

Dad then said you will come back to the ranch and you better stay for awhile

570 You need to mature a little settle down get your life in line fine a nice girl like your mother if you can find one like that.

Find one that has your best interest in mind on their own.

575 Tommy your best hustle is horse racing it's what you breathe for not snooker but you're just a good hustler.
You have a way to slow down your competition.

And every trick in the book besides I never taught you that you did that yourself.

580 My advice is to stay away from the snooker for a while.

Your hot right now.
 But you came home with over two million cash that's big money tommy.
You now have over six hundred head of cows.
585

A nice ranch, if you make more I'll by you more land.

Then Dad told tommy stay away from those politicians from Delaware or anywhere ales
590

There real hustlers.
That girl was only trouble,

What's her name "tommy "Lisa?
595 Dad then said out with the trash!

You can't trust them.
Tommy anyone that shows you can't trust them exit quickly it will only get worse.

600 Yes, Dad you told me that ever since I can remember.

Ok dad I have to go up and look at my cow's ok dad said go.

But be back at six your brother Leonard sister Doreen and Gwen will be here to see you plus uncle jack they want to hear all about the stings you pulled off in New York.

7705

Final Chapters of the Legendary Cowboy Con Man
True Story of the Legendary Cowboy Con Man Tommy Set up the Italian Mafia and took their money like they were school children.

7710

The Cowboy Con Man succeeded in creating Multitude of enemies through the years that consisted of a great many diver's faction's and gang's.

The hate was epic against the cowboy con man (REACHING WORLD WIDE)

7715 "Taking the Edge"
Tommy already had a form of the endorphins

But it was not pure it was only around six% purity the rest was old blood and trash from the sloppy separation.

7720

It really made the difference.

But on the next hustle tommy needed at lease eighty per cent purity then tommy could bet with confidence and it would enhance the horse's running performance

7725 thirty-five per cent or better.

Eighty % purity would enhance a race horse ability back to better than anytime in there racing currier.
They would run faster than any time in their past.

7730

Set new track records, tommy could sell the horse for ten times as much as the horse was worth.
Cash gambles like they were going out of style.
The management could not test for it.

7735 THIS ENDORFINS WAS A LICSENS TO STEEL.

Tommy purchased the most in-depth books the crazy man had published this man in

some ways was hundreds of years ahead of his time
 people would not reed his work but tommy did This man was HITLER- He mentioned
the endorphins and how they worked tommy was very interested and started to
Endeavour into HEAVY studying of endorphins.

 It didn't take long for tommy to discover the two main endorphins for exactly what
tommy needed (The Holy GRAIL OF SUPPER ENHANCERS.)

This would make the con man millions of dollars plus would put tommy fifty years or
more ahead of my competition
Plus, the ball and mighty food and drug act

These endorphins only had one snag.
They were only workable from human to human.

Horse to horse and were not interspecies.

"THANK YOU, MR HITLER,

Tommy had a friend that owned a horse slaughtering plant.
 Tommy made a deal to buy as many (patellar glands) as possible.

 After the horse was shot
The first thing that was done the butcher cut into the forehead of the dying horse.

Then cut out the pituitary gland in front of the brain.

 Then flash freeze it immediately
 Tommy rented a Dry ice container.

In two-month tommy had five thousand pituitary glands in the container.

Tommy was about to go where no man went before.

Tommy deeded to separate the (BATA ENDORPHINS) (KAPLAN ENDORPHINS)

THESE WERE THE MOTHER LOAD (BATA) GAVE THE HORSE AN ATHELSTIC HIGH

FEELING.

7775

THE BATA WOULD GIVE THE HORSE A FEELING OF BEEING THE BEST NOTHING SCARES HIM HE IS INVINCIBLE

7780   THE KAPLANS WERE A NATURAL PAIN KILLER TEN THOUSAND TIMES STROGER THEN MORPHIN.
They were imposable to test for there is a blood brain barrier anything from the nerves spinal cord will not be the blood or urine or sweat.

7785   THIS COMBANATION WAS DEADLY.

Then Tommy heard a 4th year chemical
Student to separate the Kaplan and Bata endorphins and get at least eighty percent purity
7790   This was successful tommy was armed with the (HOLLY GRAIL ENHANCERS)

No one could match tommy now tommy is now the most dangerous horse trainer in the world with this magic.
Tommy now could set up the Italian bookies and all the rest of the world bookie joints;
7795
Eighty percent purity
Which were seventy per cent stronger then what he was using?

Tommy had to now find the right horse then fucking nail the bookies.
7800
There was an old friend that never used any drugs of any kind on his horses.

He had an old ten-year-old horse call river snake he was raised in a swamp and could not run on a fast track could not win against bottom claimers on a fast track.
7805
But when it rained came and the worse the race trace was the better old snake could run.
Old snake could beat twenty-thousand-dollar horse in the mud.
Lucky for tommy it never rained all year in Alberta Canada.
7810

Tommy was drinking coffee with his friend and said how much for old snake.

His friend said it never rained this year and old snake cost too much to train him and wait for the rain I am looking for black clouds every day.

15

Tommy answered I know.
 But you run the old horse for three thousand claiming that's the lowest he could run for and can't win.
 It looks like old snake was finished his age ten years old within two months he would turn eleven years old tommy said?

20

I'll give you twenty-five hundred right now.

 Nope he said I want thirty-five hundred for old snake.

25 Tommy smiled at his friend and pulled the three thousand cash out his pocket.
There you are tommy said.
Ok take that son of a bitch only run in the mud.

Thanks tommy I was getting a little short anyway gets that old son of a bitch out of

30 here.
Tommy got the horse he wanted;
There was a race track in sanfrancico called bay meadows it always rained there all winter all winter long.
 While in Calgary tommy was Introducing to a beautiful blond called Darlene

35

She was from a family in west Calgary only child. (She loved horses)
Man, she was a spitting image of Maryland Munroe.

Darlene was very interested in racing horse's that made it easy for tommy to talk to

40 her. Tommy spent all day with her at stamped park;

 Darlene was a good horse handicapper. (We fit like a pair of gloves)

Darlene was an eminent girl she did not know about the world of deceit.

45

 Darlene only had good intentions in her heart.

But she was the sexiest and the prettiest girl tommy had ever met.

7850   They both did not want to leave each other,
        So, they went to the western night club called the ranchmen.
        We started drinking in the front lounge.

        Then went back to the saddle room where the live band was playing.
7855   IT WAS decorated with champion saddles plus tommy old friends chuck wagon tied to
        the ceiling of the saddle room, Ward Willard's winning the Calgary stampede.

        Tommy and Darlene fell in love right there.
        With an old cowboy sing Mr. Wayne Void.
7860   And Ian Tyson singing (summer wages)
        One of his big hits (At that time)

        Darlene and tommy stayed at the bow valley delta.
        For three days.
7865   Then the deal was they stayed together until the proper time to merry

        Darlene had to return home to get her belongings and then came and met tommy at
        Stampede Park take in the races then get ready to ship river snake to California.
        Tommy hired and old man as a groom to look after old snake.
7870

        Old cliff was the best care taker at Stampede Park.
        And worked for tommy for years old cliff liked to drink beer all day and night.

        Old cliff knew tommy and said tommy was the luckiest trainer on earth all the other
7875   horses would all fall accept tommy was the luckiest trainer cliff ever seen
        As cliff sipped on a beer
        Cliff was ready to load snake into the horse trailer and head for bay meadows
        sanfrancico California.

7880   Darlene was hurrying and asks tommy would you leave me.
        Tommy wicked and said I know you would be heir quickly but you just made it.

        We all got into the pickup truck and headed south to sweet grass Montana.
        The Canada and USA boarder

385   It didn't take long to get through into the United States.

When leaving the boarder old cliff said he would ride with the horse in the horse
trailers front tack room.
   Tommy said ok if that's what you want to get in then as cliff entered tommy shut the
390 horse trailer door.

In five hours' tommy pulled in to a gas station while filling with gas tommy checked on
old cliff.
Tommy opened the door and their old cliff was sitting grinning and said everything is
95 really good;
Cliff was drunk and drinking more cliff stored lots of beer in the horses tack box.

Darlene and tommy went in and ordered supper and for cliff.
On the way, out tommy opened the tack room door and put cliff's supper inside for
00 when he gets hungry.
Tommy told Darlene that old cliff stashed the beer in there the night before.

The next morning tommy and Darlene could heir cliff kicking the trailer door to get out
of that confined place.
05   Darlene said stop Tommy cliff wants out.
   Tommy said in a while Darlene.
The next time old cliff might think before he does this again?

   Passing cars were all pointing at the trailer door.
10 Tommy would smile and nod.
Tommy never stopped until six that night cliff only kicked the door for two hours.

Then tommy stopped and opened the trailer door.

15 Old cliff was sleeping the beer off.
   So, tommy shut the door again
And we drove straight through the night to bay meadows race track.

Tommy drove to the barn and woke up cliff.
20 Then tommy walked snake around and bath snake in shampoo snake shipped good.

Then walked snake until he was dried by this time cliff had snakes stall ready.

In snake went and tommy took off his halter, snake lay down and stretched out on his
7925   side.
He was a smart horse.
Then cliff had a hot mash for snake to eat snake jumped up and eat the whole mash.
This was a good sign.
Darleen was apartment hunting.
7930   Old cliff and tommy went to the race track kitchen.

There were lots of good horse trainers there with very expensive horses.
Tommy new most of them but declined to talk.
The lowest key is the best road for the cowboy right now.
7935

Old cliff started telling tommy this only fucking horse you got heir and this horse is a
fucking cheap bum.

Did you forget where we are tommy cliff said?
7940

We are in California the hardest racing in America.
Tommy has you lost your fucking marbles.

That old river snake is eleven years old and can't win for bottoms in Calgary.
7945

Tommy you're crazy.
"Tommy said cliff just sit and wait I have something ells in mind.

O k CLIFF SAID BUT I AM EMBAREST!
7950   Tommy said please look after snake good please.

Yes, cliff agreed but then said that horse is a pig (tommy)

Darleen rented apartment and we left the track. Tommy told cliff to walk snake
7955   tomorrow I will come the next day.

Tommy was tired and when we walk into the small apartment the first thing was a
shower.

Then straight to bed with the sexiest woman on earth

60

Three weeks went by still no rain
 But old snake was really training great with all the muscle builders and vitamins;
His hair was starting to shine like silk.
Then tommy had to work old River snake six furlongs.

65

Then used a small shot of endorphins just to see if it would help

Well the ten-year-old worked fast six furlongs in 1.12 it was the fastest workout of the day.

70   Under a good hold by the exercise rider
 When dismounting the exercise rider was asking what's the name of this horse.
Tommy ignored the rider

Well tommy said to cliff now what do you think.

75

Old cliff was sure prized.
 But said racing is different than work outs then added snake is a pig!
He never wins a race in three years.
But tommy watched old snake just work faster than hundred-thousand-dollar horse.

80

The pure endorphins are working on that old horse maid old snake young again.

Instead of being over tiered snake had a bow in his neck and his tail over raised his back?

85   Meaning he was happy no stress.
 Loved what he just did.
 Snake was ready.
Snake will win when the rain comes snake is a soupier muddier:
Improve in the bud one thousand times.

90   Now tommy is going to get ready for it the sting.

Tommy had time for the set up now Tommy called fast eddy in Lethbridge Alberta.

Asked if he would go place some bets for tommy and get paid on a per cent age.

95

Like the old times.

Eddy answered you bet where you are.

Tommy said fly into sanfrancico.

 And I'll pay eddy for the air ticket when you get here.

8000 "Eddy said right now

"Tommy said as fast as possible!

"Ok fast eddy said I am on the first thing smoking.

Tommy went back to the apartment and told Darleen about a (real sleaze bag) Called

Fast Eddy who is coming down to help place my money in eastern USA on old river

8005 snake.

Darleen ask how much are you going to bet tommy.

Tommy said around twenty-five thousand or more.

8010 Tommy said as much as they will take.

Darleen said wow.

 Is this not tommy but that cowboy con man talking now and smiled.

8015 "Tommy said please don't ever say that again the cowboy con man is not welcome

anywhere!

In fact, we are going to the race track and turn over river snake to you Darleen you're

the owner of river snake.

8020 And cliff will get his trainer's license.

Cliff is your training Darleen.

 Don't tell fast eddy the name of the horse.

 There is no Cowboy Con man involved.

8025 "Darleen said but it's the cowboy's setup.

Fast eddy called tommy the next night.

Well I am at the airport.

 Tommy gave eddy the apartment address take a cab.

8030 Eddy said on my way.

Eddy was asking what the name of the horse.

"Tommy said I'll let you know.
After you play the duck and start losing cash set those eastern bookies up.

35

Eddy asks where I am going.
"Tommy said fly to Chicago then take a bus to Gary Indiana set them up lose money for a few days.

40   That town is full of bookies.
Then when we run
Try and bet as much as they will take on the head end to win?
 Eddy said no back up.
Tommy said small but most on the front end this horse is going to win or run up the
45   track.
EDDY said ok.
 Then tommy said then flies to Delaware.
 Brown town it a part of Wilmington It's full of bookies.

50   Ok eddy said tell me when.
 Tommy said this horse is a superior bud runner;
We have to wait until it starts to rain
Tommy said you should be able to place twenty-five thousand easily without tipping your hat.
55   Ok Eddy you leave tomorrow and start losing $200.00 to $500.00 at every one of those bookies set them up eddy make the $500.00 dollar loses sound like you lose $50.000.00.
 Use what good gift your mouth.
Set them up, called padding the books.
60

Fast eddy was on the plain the next day.
 To Garry Indiana then brown town Delaware plus Atlantic City
It was six days' later and still no rain.

65   Tommy had to work old snake again make sure he was ready.
Tommy worked snake a different way this time
So, if snake worked fast it would not show.
Tommy told the exercise boy to breeze snake a mile.

8070   Then sit down and extend snake the last three furlongs.
         Old snake worked really good and never showed a fast work out?
        Snake was ready.

        We waited and watched the forecast.
8075
        And the long-range forecast said rain and lots of it in the following week.

        Eddy called and said I got both Brown town and Garry Indiana prim.

8080   They think I am the dumbest big mouth gambler they ever seen.

         Now tommy what's the name of you horse.

        Tommy answered Eddy you're not my fucking partner your deal is you take a per cent
8085   of the money you place is that the deal if not let me know right now.

        YES, Cowboy that's the deal.
         Ok tommy said I'll let you know the day of the race.

8090   " Ok eddy agreed but was saying what to fuck in the back ground.

        Tommy was now concerned about Fast Eddy.
         It wouldn't take much to fuck up this gamble.

8095   The weekend was here and there was big black rain cloud blowing in off the pacific

         It was about to storm.
        Tommy was waiting to see how much water would come.

8100   Because the race Corse was built to sustain lots of water before it would seep through
        there layer of hard pan.
         It rained for three days the track was starting to get really bad.

         Tommy picked a race to enter snake.
8105   None winners of the year for sixty-two hundred $6200.00
        Twice as much as old snake runs for.

Old Cliff entered river snake and named on a drunken rider friend of cliff.
It was a class less show with old cliff and old equipment old snake it was a bush track
show. Tommy smile, it was great old cliff had only three black teeth and his jockey had
10   less. No one would pay them any attention.

THE BETING AND HANDILING "FAST EDDY

Tommy called eddy, "Tommy asked when can you place the bets' can stumble in and
do it tomorrow do it and I will call you when both brown town and Garry Indiana are
15   down and Atlantic City.
The name of the horse that might not win is River snake.

A ten-year-old that" never won for three years.

20   Eddy then said I thought this was a real gamble.

 How can you bet on that pig?
"Tommy told Fast Eddy he probably gets beat but I am gambling Fuck I am not betting
on that fucking Alberta pig fast eddy said.
25

The next afternoon eddy called and said it's done and I think you just gave your money
away tommy.
Yes, tommy said this is a long shot.

30   Eddy said I'll bring the tickets or the cash to you later.

You give me my per cent; even if you lose bring the old tickets tommy said.

I'll have your cash; Eddy Said I am not interested in placing even one dollar of my
35   money on that pig and I was almost respecting you Cowboy.

Ok Tommy said get you air plane ticket to sanfrancico.
Day of the race
, I'll remember you heir.
40   Tommy administrated the endorphins snake was reacting so well.

It hit him almost endemically snake was really high on himself.

Started playing and still had that eye of a champion ready to do battle full of
8145   confidents you could see it all over him.
The races were starting.
River snake was in the third race.
Tommy told Darleen and cliff that they would not see Tommy at the race track today.

8150   I'll meet you Darleen back at the apartment late at night.

The Cowboy can't be around your guys or there could be trouble.

Then Darleen started talking about how smart Fast Eddy must be flying east and
8155   tricking those bookie guys and betting old snake.

Tommy was surprised at this entire talk about all the excitement about Fast Eddy.
And ignored it?

8160   Tommy went to the bottom of the grandstand set in the cheapest sets.

"Waited for river snakes race."

8165   Then the horses were on a short post parade because of the rain down pour the horse
stayed in the paddock until post time then went straight to the starting gate.

Tommy got in line to the fifty-dollar ticket window. Snacks odds was 99 to 1

8170   Tommy dropped three thousand to win and three thousand to place.

There were 30 seconds tell the betting windows would close.

If anyone seen the six thousand dollars' tommy just dropped on snake
8175   It would be too late for anyone to betony thirty seconds left.

Then walked away from everyone to watch old snake run in the mud for his last race

The bookies had a limit of what they had to pay when a horse shows 99 to 1.

80   That horse was going to pay up to one thousand dollars to one.

       The standard top pays off for bookies is seventy too one.

85   Tommy was betting at the track to get the over odds that the bookie was not going to pay off on.

       Tommy would collect big if snake wins.

90   The flag was up; they were about to start old snake was number 12

       Away on the outside were the track would be better than the rail.

       There off and running the announcer started then started calling the horses and River
95   snake was laying third and the rider pulled snake to the outside and set down and let snake run.
       River snake circled the field then went to the front easily then they were at the half mile pole River snake opening up on the field.
       Down the lane they come, river snake had a commanding lead.
00
       Winner by eighteen lengths
       Darleen and old cliff were standing in the winner's circle both as happy as two pigs in shit.
       Tommy waited around the stairs until the price was listed then.
05
       TOMMY WITH AND OLD HAT ON WITH SUN GLASS 'S, CASHED THE SIX THOUSAND DOLLARS OF TICKETS.

       Tommy collected over $167.000.00.and tommy ran out the front entrance of the
10   grandstand.
        And keep running until he was completely away from their though a park and over the freeway bridge.
       Tommy made sure nobody was following.
        And it was a clear getaway from the racetrack officials they were all sleeping.
15
        But when they figure this out things will get hot!

Best thing is to be miles away and time away from these people.

8220   We will move snake before ten thirty tomorrow morning.

Then took a cab to the apartment
Hide the cash in his suit case.
 Then waited for Eddy to call and Darleen to get back to the apartment
8225

The phone rang it was Fast Eddy wall cowboy you showed me again.
How do you do this tommy?
This is the third time you pulled a sneaky one off on me.

8230   "Tommy asks Eddy have you cashed in the tickets in brown town. "Yes, Eddy said I am
flying in one hour to Garry Indiana I have already called them they know they got
fucked and are asking questions about that cowboy con man.
 . I don't even know you.
 But keep you head up,
8235   You better not show up around the race track?

 Then FAST EDDY SAID HE WAS BOOKED ON A RED EYE to sanfrancico is there at four
thirty in the morning.

8240   Tommy said Eddy take a cab to the apartment. Bring the cash ho I know you would get
around to that.
 Tommy just said see you at five I'll leave the front door open.

Then Darleen came in with beer smell and said cliff is in the truck.
8245   Tommy said good bring him in old cliff walked in and was grinning man old snake sure
run a good one didn't he tommy.

Tommy told cliff too set down and have something to eat because you have to take the
truck and hock the trailer up and load all your things and load snake up and get out of
8250   bay meadows before six in the morning.
Cliff said I can't do that.
Tommy said you stop your fucking drinking and be professional and get snake out of
there now go to the office at six in the morning get the papers bring them to me and

Darlene will sign snake over to you and you can have that truck and horse trailer. It's all
255 yours pulse I'll give you two thousand dollars too.
Cliff get out of here go to Arizona.
 Remove all evidence.
 Leave and take snake with you.
 Oak cliff answered but cliff did not like it.
260 You mean leave right now.
 Yes, tommy said get snakes papers on the way out no later they 6:30. Get going cliff.
Old cliff went to the stable all worried about the track security and those federal
agents.
Darleen was real anxious to meet Fast Eddy. She said eddy is so smart. He's the Con
265 man. In walks, fast eddy
Then when he seen the cowboy eddy.
Then said tommy hires your cash and I never touched a cent of it.

Tommy counted it there was two hundred and thirty thousand there.
70 Tommy has made close to four hundred thousand.

Tommy quickly counted out forty thousand dollars.
FAST EDDY SAID Cowboy your word is good.

75 Thank you just let me know what's up the next hustle.

Darleen ask fast eddy if he had a card then eddy gave Darleen his card there was an
innocent picture of fast eddy with a small tear drop and a grave stone.

80 It was eddy's front he was selling coffins and grave stones.

Then tommy looked at eddy and said   why don't you take Darleen home with you
fast eddy said Darleen I know not to fool with the cowboy's ladies

85 Tommy told Darleen we are flying.

But Darleen was still shining up to fast eddy.
Tommy was about to leave Darleen when Eddy said please Darleen you're going to get
me killed.
90 Then eddy left he know the meeting was over.

After eddy left tommy asked Darleen you like Fast eddy hay.

Darleen Looked Tommy strait in the eye and said he is an interesting character tommy.

Now tommy said that bothers me Darleen. "Darleen said why I am not that interested

8295 in him that way?

Stop that tommy.

Tommy said through his card away,

Darleen crumpled it up and put the card in the ash tray. AFFER MENORISING EDDYS ADRESS AND PHONE NUMBER.

8300

(THIS IS THE END OF THE COWBOY CON MAN)
PLEASE REED THE CONTINUING STORY OF THE
(COWBOY CON MAN TWO) GLORY YEAR WERE TO COME EVEN
BETTER THAN THE GREAT ONE HIMSELF THE GREAT Gatsby &other

8305 world con man.

"(THE LEGENDARY COWBOY CON MAN –TWO-)"

The cowboy con man was well known as a dirty aggravating deadly con man.

The con man had to retreat to the ranch and become a rancher,

8310   or get killed the greasers the Italians were aggravated.

Tommy had a nice ranch with a full heard of cow's tommy had a nice yearly income from the ranch.

Tommy now had to stay out of hustler's ally or tommy would be killed. Nobody likes to

315 be conned.

Tommy had to stay on the ranch or find a way to rise above his enemies.
Darleen was not in love with tommy, she was in love with the cowboy con man.
When tommy became a rancher, Darleen got restless and became unfaithful and full of
320 lies thanking she could con the con man.

It was Dangerous for the cowboy con man,
it wasn't the money tommy won it was the lying and cheating way's tommy set them
up. Bull shitting the bookies put up titles of old horse trailers for betting credit the
325 cowboy never even had to put up any cash. Plus, there wasn't even any real trailer
there was only useless paper titles, the con man knows they would never be used!

The Italian mafia bookies were mad at the con job. How did that sun of a bitch get to us
that fucking easy?
330 They were going to get their money back or the fucking cowboy con man would
disappear.
The conman was looked at by the bookies as a thief lyre the lowest the lowest form of
human life.
The Italians were mad!!
335 The con man replied from a distance, ITS OK FOR YOU GREASERS to take people's
houses, but when you get it back your sore losers!
Fuck you greasers the cowboy said.
"As tommy crossed the international border into Canada, 145 miles from the ranch and
built in family safety with a pocket full of cash. Enough to buy another four hundred
340 head of cows plus.
Nothing moved up in those hills without everyone knowing about it, I flicker of a light
nothing got through.
We all looked after each other; the whole ranch community was armed.
No strangers were welcome until we let them.
345 What a wonderful place.
Darlene was never aware of the country organization. These hills were smart and very
capable people and close. This use to be home stead land of the west. And it's away
from any ware gangsters running away from the law mafia found their homes, and we
weren't any different.
350

THANK'S FOR READING